INVESTING IN OIL in the '80s

WITHOUT SPENDING A FORTUNE

INVESTING IN OIL IN THE '80s

WITHOUT SPENDING A FORTUNE

Paul Garrison

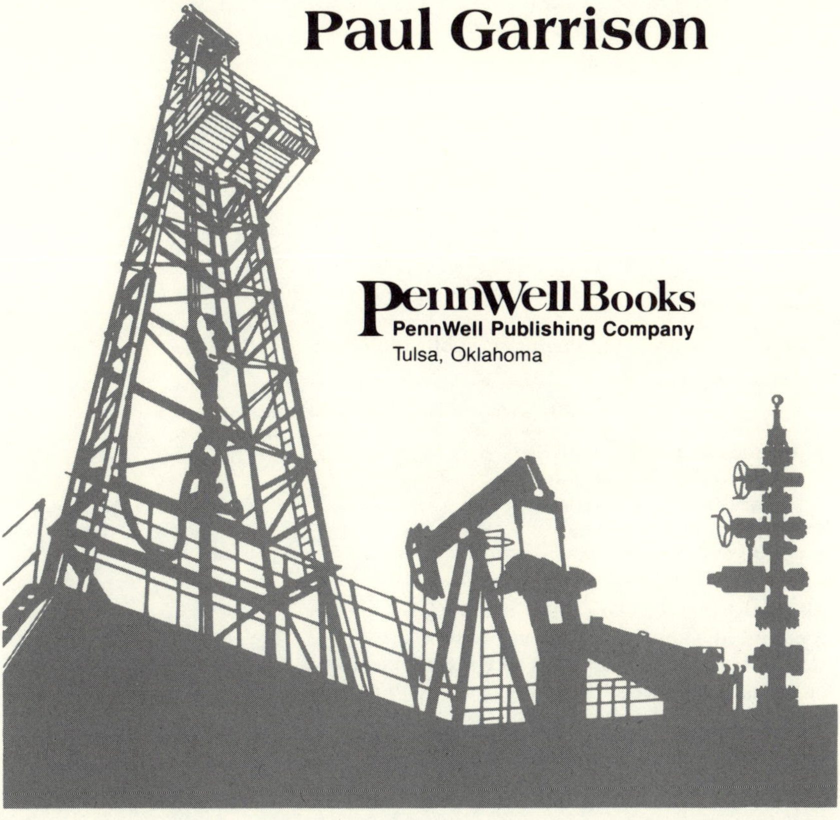

PennWell Books
PennWell Publishing Company
Tulsa, Oklahoma

1421 South Sheridan Road/P. O. Box 1260
Tulsa, Oklahoma 74101

Library of Congress Cataloging in Publication Data

Garrison, Paul.
Investing in oil in the '80s without spending a fortune.

Includes index.
1. Petroleum industry and trade—Finance.
2. Investments. I. Title.
HD9560.5.G38 332.63 80-39731
ISBN 0-87814-151-0

Printed in the United States of America

2 3 4 5 85 84 83 82

Dedication

This book is dedicated to the independent oil operators and investors who individually and collectively have made and continue to make a major contribution toward finding and supplying gas and oil for our country.

As long as our free enterprise system and American entrepreneurs can prevail against government controls, taxes, and regulations, I believe we can become independent of foreign oil supplies.

For their assistance and generous cooperation, the author is in the debt of a number of people whose knowledge, experience, and encouragement provided the foundation of this book. A partial list includes Jack Womack, Warren Johnston, Cloyce Talbot, Charles Walker, Ed Thompson, C. H. Browning, Kenneth Hankins, Wanema Howard and Gorman Webb.

Paul Garrison

Contents

Introduction

Hard work will usually provide an adequate living; in fact, during a lifetime of productive endeavor, the average person earns over $1 million. We work and save to achieve a degree of financial security, but real security—the kind which results in continuing, effortless income—can be obtained only if we use some of that earned money in carefully selected investment opportunities.

There are, of course, many such opportunities. People have made money by investing in the stock market. Others owe their financial success to profitable speculations in real estate. Still others have bought paintings, art objects, and precious gems and metals in the belief that their value will rise more rapidly than the rate of inflation. Classic cars, antiques, and stamp and coin collections constitute investments. In fact, there is always the opportunity to use savings or funds borrowed from banks to begin a business, hoping for meaningful financial rewards.

And then there is oil. Oil is unique; it offers a way for the average person to convert a limited amount of risk capital into a regular income rather than into a one-time profit. Today, the opportunities are greater than they have ever been. Even with relatively limited capital resources, you can become part of the oil boom of the 1980s. You may not become an overnight millionaire, although this has happened, but the chances of ending up with a healthy monthly check for the rest of your life are within reach. That's the route I decided to take.

In the old days, it was par for the course to put money away for a specific purpose. But we're no longer used to saving first and buying later for cash. In these days of credit cards and interest rates, our entire existence is attuned to buying now and paying later. But you should never buy into an oil well on credit. Since that's what I had decided to do, I had to adjust my thinking and discipline myself to a systematic program of putting money aside.

Not knowing anyone who was actively involved in the oil business I read everything on the subject that I could get my hands on. Based on this knowledge, I felt I would need to accumulate $15,000 which wouldn't be needed for any other purpose. When I finally collected the money, I contacted a friend's friend who knew someone who, as he put it, dabbled in oil. A letter of introduction and several long-distance phone calls later, I was on an airplane to Dallas and finally getting actively involved in that business which had occupied so much of my thinking for so long.

I met my contact at the airport and we transferred to a small, single-engine plane. I watched him do the customary preflight check, and a few minutes later we were climbing out into the somewhat hazy sky, heading west toward Midland and Odessa.

"Nice," I said, thinking what a delight it was not to have to deal with metal detectors or be stuck with inconvenient airline schedules.

"Sure is. She's the first thing I bought when my first well came in."

"Your well?"

"Well, not really. All I have of it is one percent, and I tell you frankly, I was sweating it when it was being drilled. It was the sixth one I'd put money into. All the others, all five, had been dry holes, and I wasn't sure if I'd have enough left to try again if this one turned out to be another dud."

"I take it this one turned out all right."

"You can say that again. We've been pumping nearly a hundred barrels a day for over a year now, and since then we've hit several more times."

In the back of my mind I could already see the monthly checks coming in, hot and heavy. I knew, of course, that I was just dreaming, but why not?

We finally landed in Odessa and drove to the office. After introductions were exchanged, my friend opened up the conversation. "Bill," he said when we were all seated, "Paul is thinking of going into the oil business, but he doesn't know much about it."

"Nobody knows what it's all about. But I'll be glad to do what I can."

"I do appreciate that," I said, not knowing what else to say.

"In 1962, I got started in the well-servicing business on my own. After a while I stumbled across a prospect that looked good and then another and another, so I gradually got into the exploration and production business. Prospects, that's what it's all about. You see, the key to finding oil is having the acreage to drill on. That's where the big oil companies have the advantage. They'll lease tens of thousands of acres and they'll have as many as thirty or forty rigs going in one area. I and all the other independents, we do the same thing, only on a smaller scale. Some years I'll drill as few as two or three wells, and others maybe seven or eight. It all depends on finding the right prospects and then being able to lease the land."

"Do you do that all yourself, or do you have some antennas out there?"

"Both. What I could really use is a good geologist. The good ones, the oil finders, seem to go consistently where there is oil. It has to do with an analytical mind. They can visualize what went on down there under the ground and they somehow know what constitutes a trap and where to find it. There are many places where you get into some pretty complicated geology. The deeper the structure, the more analytical you have to be."

He got up and walked over to one of the maps on the wall.

"The way I found this prospect right here, that's really funny. I'd been looking at it for years and Olin had drilled this pretty good well right here. One day, I get a call, telling me that they plugged that well. So one Sunday I drove up there because I wanted to make sure that I knew what was going on.

"Anyway, in looking it over I find that this land was open over on this side. It somehow seems logical that if it's good over there, it should be good over here, too. So I checked around and found out who the landowner was and called her up. She had gotten $50 an acre and a straight eighth lease. However, she hadn't gotten her lease back yet. Anyway, she told me that they had two more weeks to go before the thirty-day deadline. So in the meantime I did some more checking and found that a well on this adjoining acreage has produced over 190,000 barrels so far and the one they junked had produced over 200,000 barrels before they plugged it. I really felt that I wanted this deal. I talked to this lady on the day when thirty days were up and the lease hadn't come back. So I told her I'd give her $100 an acre on a straight eighth lease or $50 an acre on a three-sixteenths lease. And I told her that we'd have the money over there the next day. Anyway, to make a long story short, those other guys had missed their deadline and I got the lease for $100 an acre for three years with a straight eighth royalty. That's one way you play the game."

"And that got you started."

"That well has paid for a lot of mistakes over the years. Most of the drilling I do is close in, like what we call 'in the shadow of the derrick.' I do very little true exploration work. That's what most of the independents do, though some get involved in some real wildcatting. And everything I do I do with partners, often as many as thirty-five. I've got a whole list of people who expect me to automatically include them in every deal. Sometimes I actually end up with less percentage for myself, simply because there is always one more investor who wants to get in on the deal. A lot of them take only one or one-and-a-half percent, and when they want in I don't like to turn anyone down. Most of them are people I know, and we're not talking about big bucks, maybe a thousand or fifteen hundred is all."

"Is it smarter to invest more money in fewer wells, or less money in a greater number?"

"As I said, I've got people who automatically want in for one or two percent of everything I do. That's the smart way to do it, because there just isn't anybody alive who can pick just the one deal that'll come in. If you go around picking and choosing, first thing you know you'll throw up your hands because you've picked all the dry holes, and one good deal will pay for ten bad ones."

"Tell me, where do you find the people to buy the oil or gas from you when you do find it?"

"I don't find them. They find me. Any time I get started on a well, I get calls and letters from oil and gas buyers. It's the easiest thing in the world to find people to buy the oil. The trick is finding it in the first place."

"How much money would it really take?" I was thinking of my $15,000 and by now I was just about ready to hand it over and tell him to spread it around over as many deals as he could.

"There are a lot of people who'll say to themselves, 'Oh, what the hell. I'll play $1,500 and see what happens.' That's like going to

Vegas and throwing it on the roulette table and hoping your number comes up. If you're going to play the game, you've got to think in terms of averages. Some come in, a lot don't. What you should do is go to whomever you want to invest with and find out how many wells he'll be drilling over, say, the next year, and then you should spread whatever money you have to invest over all those wells, buy a small piece of every well. All you need is one good one in the bunch, and it'll pay for all the others."

By the time I was ready to leave, I felt that I had received quite an education. As might have been expected, my $15,000 continued to burn a hole in my pocket, so I made my pitch and Bill agreed to count me in on whatever deals might come along for one percent each for as long as my money would last.

Now, I'm hooked. But I didn't jump in recklessly. I did a lot of research and talked to all kinds of oil people. That's what this book is all about—teaching you about oil and oil investments so you'll have better odds when you hit the table.

1

Oil–what it is and where it's found

The word *petroleum* is derived from the Latin *petra* for rock and *oleum* for oil—rock oil. Imprecise though it may be, subterranean rock formations are vital to the science of finding oil.

Oil is a fossil fuel, originating from living matter which millions, if not billions, of years ago was inundated by a series of floods that covered large sections of what is now dry land, creating an earth which consisted largely of unending oceans. To this day, if you fly low over certain portions of land such as the high plateau of northern New Mexico and the caprock of the Texas Panhandle, the shapes of the ground seen below are typical of those which would have been shaped by large bodies of water. Finally, the waters receded and the decaying fossil material was covered with layers of sand, rock, mud, limestone, and debris. The process of decay continued under the immense pressure of all that solid material, eventually producing the substances which we now know as oil and natural gas.

If, throughout all of this time, the earth had sat quite still with no earthquakes or volcanic eruptions, this oil and gas might actually have remained in a few immense, ocean-sized pools which would certainly have simplified recovery in modern times. But our earth refuses to sit calmly and quietly. Instead, its crust, the earth's surface, is in constant motion, causing all manner of subterranean and occasionally surface dislocations. In the process, those potentially large pools or oceans of oil have been pushed around, shoved upward, down, and sideways, causing them to divide into what might best be described as millions of small puddles. Granted, some of these puddles extend for hundreds of miles, but by far the largest

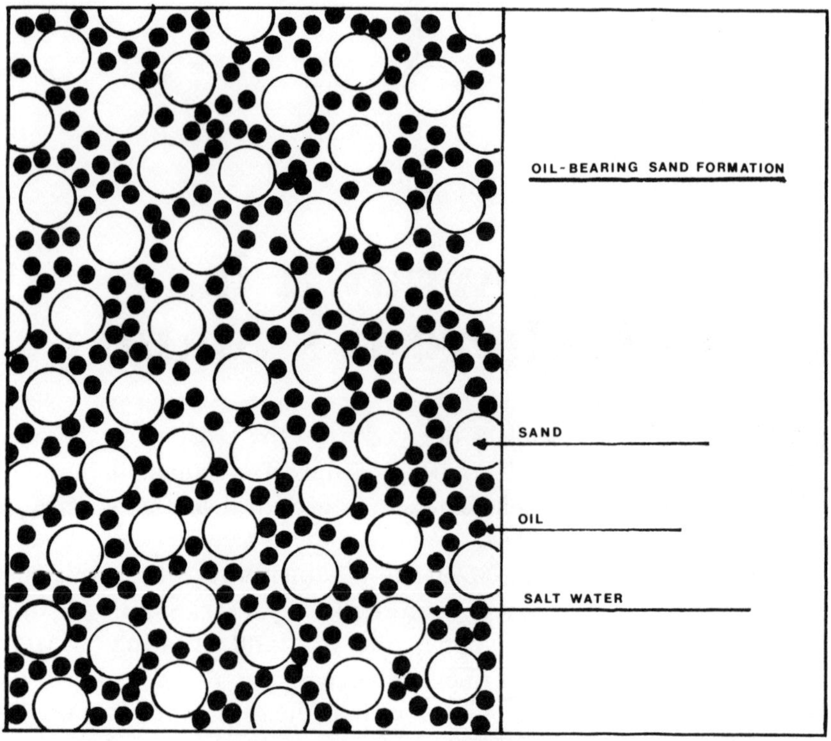

Most oil is contained in pockets of sand into which oil has seeped.

amount of the oil is contained in small pools bordered by nonporous rocks. These pools, more often than not, are not actual pools in the sense of open, underground ponds; rather, they are tiny droplets of oil and gas encased in pockets of oil-bearing sand.

Of all the nonsolid material below the surface of the earth, the largest quantity is water, and below a certain depth all of this is salt water. Oil, being lighter than water, will always tend to float to the surface. Thus, oil and gas will tend to continue rising until they are obstructed by some type of solid, impenetrable material, such as a salt dome. If no such obstruction is encountered, they will eventually seep to the surface, as in Pennsylvania where this seepage sparked the beginning of oil exploration.

By studying what can be learned from producing wells as well as dry holes, geologists have come up with a number of principles with

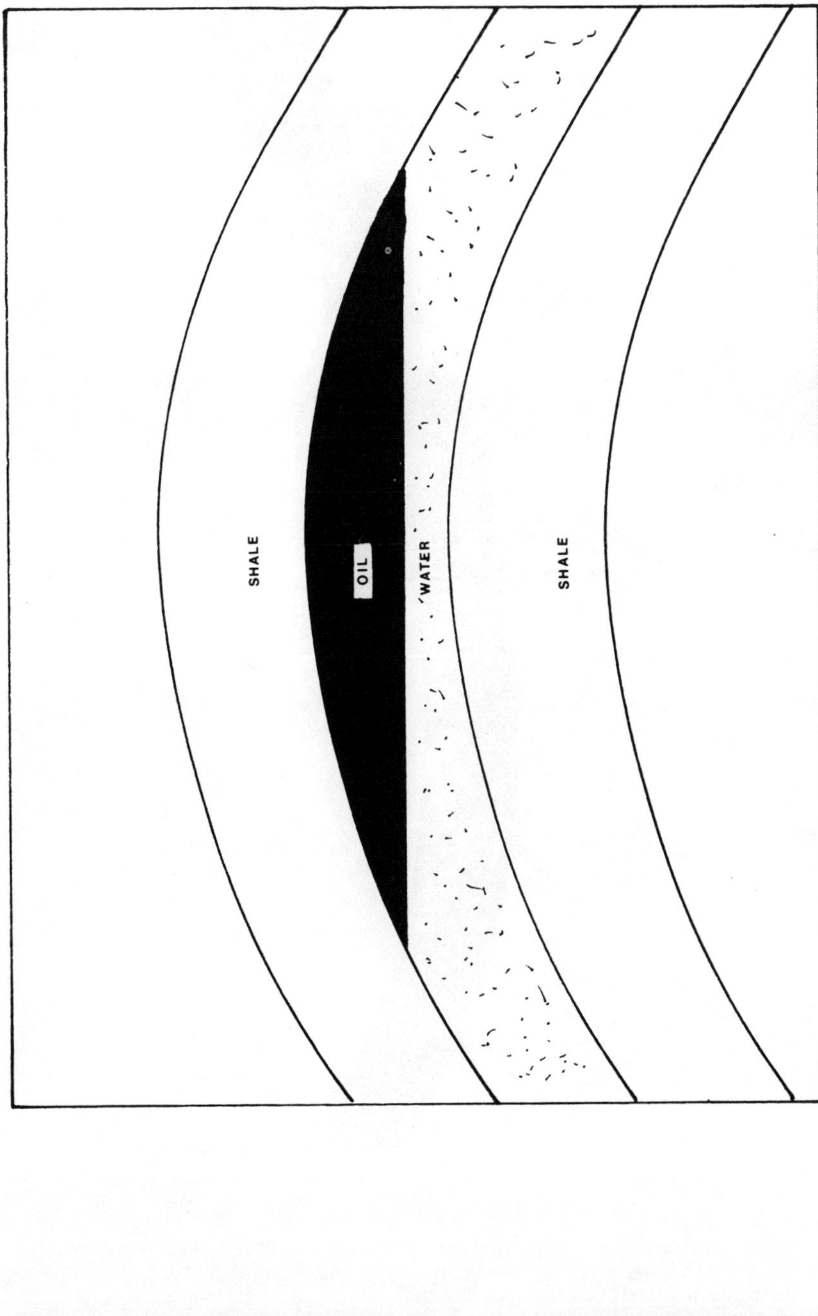

Oil is lighter than water and it tends to rise until it is obstructed by some type of solid, impenetrable material.

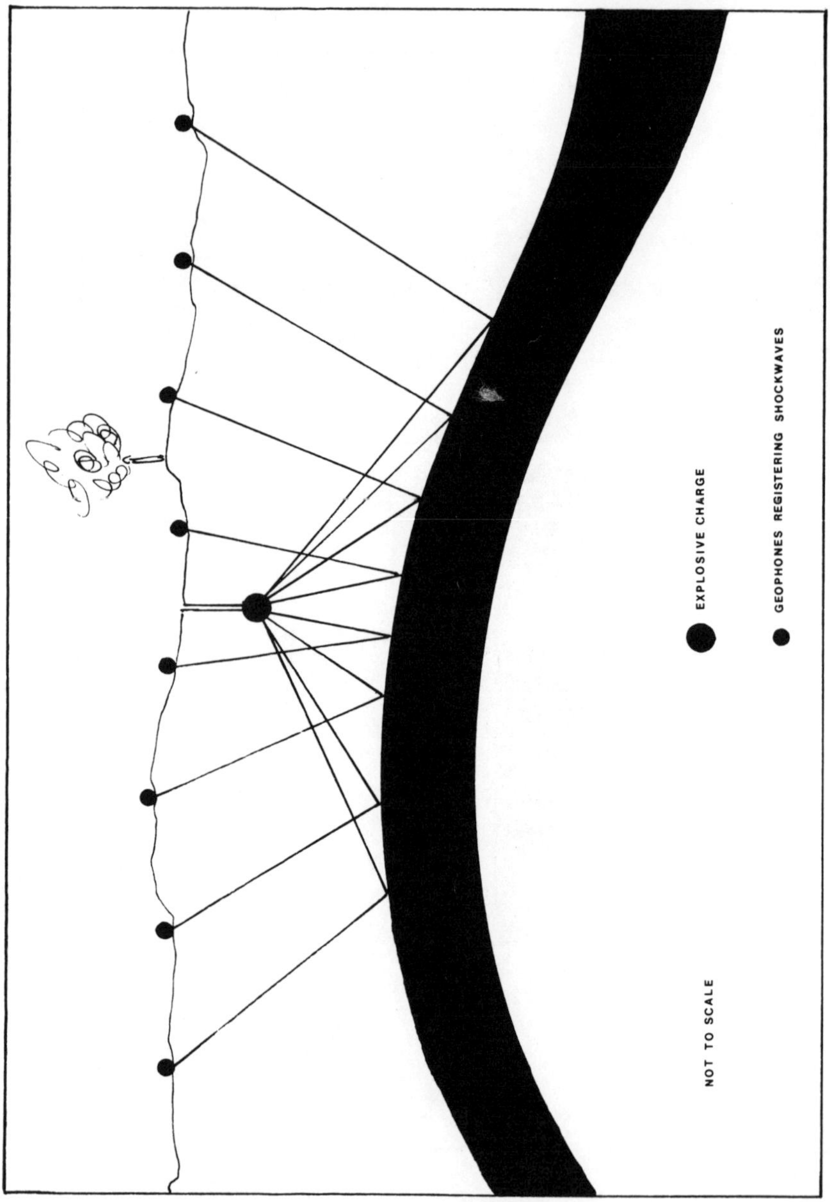

Geologists have devised a technique which utilizes the known behavior of reflected sound to determine what lies beneath the surface of the earth.

regard to subterranean rock formations which they believe to be indicative of the potential presence of oil. They have devised a variety of techniques to determine the presence of such formations, the most popular and frequently used being seismic techniques—techniques which utilize the known behavior of reflected sound to determine what lies beneath the surface. But geological science, much like forecasting the weather, is really more an art than a science, meaning that intuition, guesswork, and luck play about as much a part in the conclusions as scientific evidence. There have been repeated instances, some quite recently, when groups of highly respected geologists insisted that a certain area was devoid of any trace of oil or gas, only to be proven wrong when a few years later some stubborn cuss drilled a well and found huge reserves. Even today, with geological evidence pointing to large reserves off the Atlantic coast, wells drilled at the expense of many millions of dollars have as yet returned little profit.

No one ever knows for sure until there is an actual hole in the ground. And even then that hole may have missed oil or gas by just a few dozen feet horizontally, or the person or company drilling may have run out of optimism or funds just 50 to 100 feet above what might have turned into a meaningful find. It's strictly a gamble.

Most people believe that the only place where there is oil is in Texas, maybe Oklahoma, and, of course, in Alaska. Some may even remember that the first oil discovery in this country took place in 1859 in Pennsylvania where oil seeped out of the ground in a place that later became Oil City. But the actual story is quite different.

Take a typical month, such as January 1980. According to the *Oil and Gas Journal*, a respected and definitive publication of the oil industry, a total of 3,540 wells were drilled in that month alone in 27 states. Of these attempts at finding either oil or natural gas, 1,440 turned out to be producing oil wells, 781 were producing gas wells, and 1,243 turned out to be dry holes. (76 were so-called service wells.)

And this is just one month. Projecting these figures over a 12-month period, over 40,000 drilling projects could be expected to produce 17,300 oil wells, over 9,000 gas wells, and approximately 15,000 dry holes. Activity is continuously increasing in areas of proven reserves and also in many unexplored areas, especially

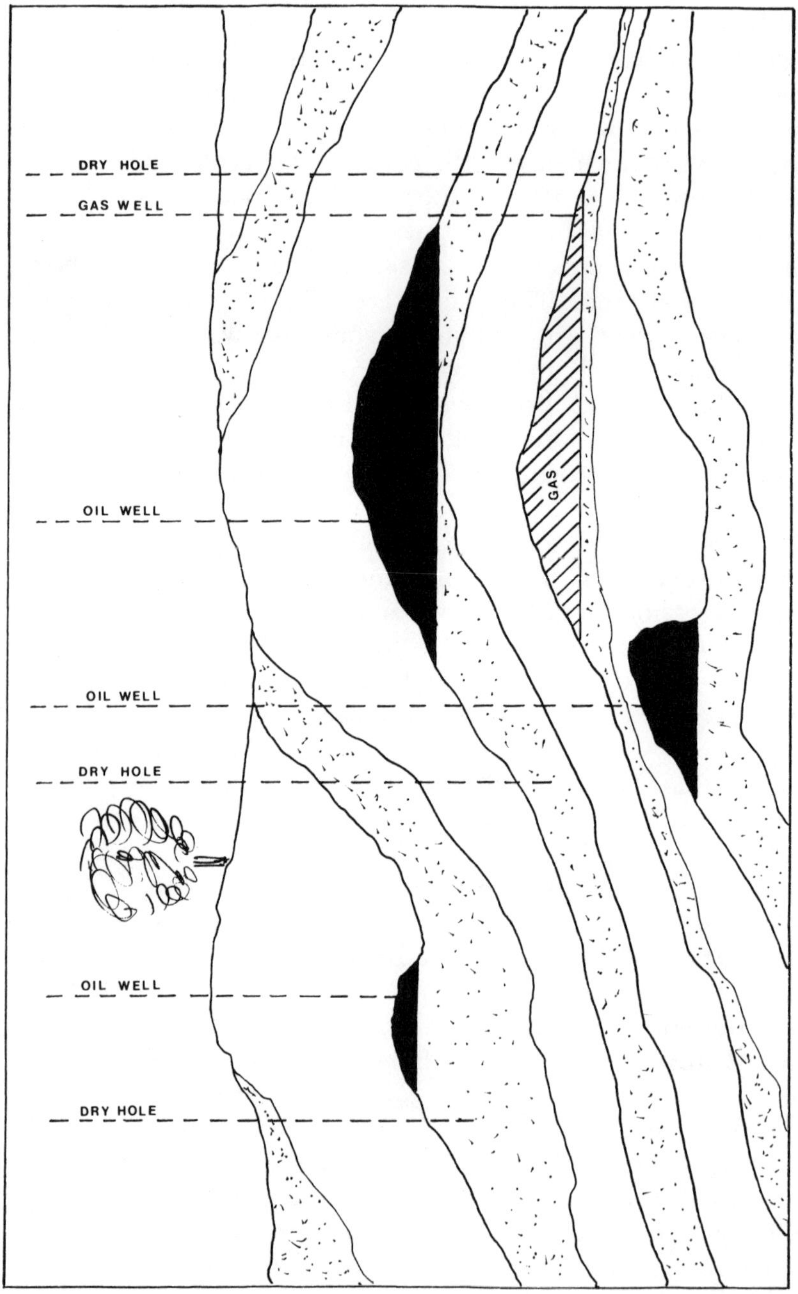

No one really knows where oil is until there is an actual hole in the ground. Even then, that hole may have missed oil or gas by just a few feet.

State	Total wells	Oil	Gas	Dry	Service
Alabama	18	1	7	10	0
Alaska	19	13	0	1	5
Arkansas	25	6	5	14	0
California	136	101	2	20	13
Colorado	62	13	12	37	0
Illinois	118	60	0	57	1
Indiana	75	27	4	44	0
Kansas	186	64	18	100	4
Kentucky	107	41	7	53	6
Louisiana	341	92	92	150	7
Michigan	58	19	2	35	2
Mississippi	51	14	3	29	5
Montana	49	9	11	28	1
Nebraska	39	12	0	27	0
Nevada	1	0	0	1	0
New Mexico	86	20	50	16	0
New York	13	1	12	0	0
North Dakota	21	16	0	5	0
Ohio	50	21	28	1	0
Oklahoma	460	230	99	131	0
Pennsylvania	60	2	58	0	0
South Dakota	1	0	0	1	0
Tennessee	20	7	9	4	0
Texas	1,354	642	240	444	28
Utah	14	4	6	4	0
West Virginia	105	2	99	4	0
Wyoming	70	23	17	26	4

along the eastern and western overthrust belts, geological formations which occur in Virginia/West Virginia and roughly along the Continental Divide from Canada to Mexico.

Most oilmen today, basing their judgment on the fact that the increased price of crude has turned previously unprofitable areas into profitable ones, have raised their estimate of the total amount of recoverable oil and natural gas in this country by several 100 percent. Many of these areas will eventually attract some enterprising wildcatter. There may never have been a derrick within hundreds of miles of where you live, but it's a safe bet that someday there will be.

In other words, we know what oil is and we will continue to find thousands of ways in which to use it for the production of energy or in the manufacture of an unlimited variety of products. We know it's down there somewhere, but we still haven't come up with a reliable solution to the question of exactly where.

2

The anatomy of a well

First of all let's get the terminology straight. A completed drilling project which has resulted in the discovery and production of oil or gas is a *well*. One which has discovered and produced nothing (other than possibly salt water) is a *dry hole*. Still, we tend to talk about drilling a well rather than a hole, which may be because you've got to be an optimist to be involved in oil or gas exploration in the first place.

Drilling a well is expensive business. At today's prices, depending on the type of ground which has to be negotiated and, to some extent, on the amount of luck which prevents minor or major mishaps from occurring, the drilling cost will run from $30 to $60 a foot. With few wells ever productive at depths of less than 1,000 feet, we can quickly see how that can add up to a lot of loot. (The first producing well ever, drilled in Pennsylvania, was dug to a depth of 69½ feet. Today some of the deepest wells have been drilled to depths of close to 30,000 feet or six miles, vertically.) But why is poking a hole in the ground so expensive? To understand the reason, let's look at what an actual well consists of.

First a derrick is erected. In the old days, they were permanent wooden structures which remained in place even after the well started producing. Today, jackknife derricks are preferred. They are portable and, once the drilling activity has ceased, are removed and used again at the next location. Their primary purpose is to provide a means of raising the lengths of drilling pipe vertically above the hole into which they have to be fed. They also contain all of the primary drilling machinery. Additional equipment consists of draw works, motors, mud pumps, and a seemingly endless variety of accessories.

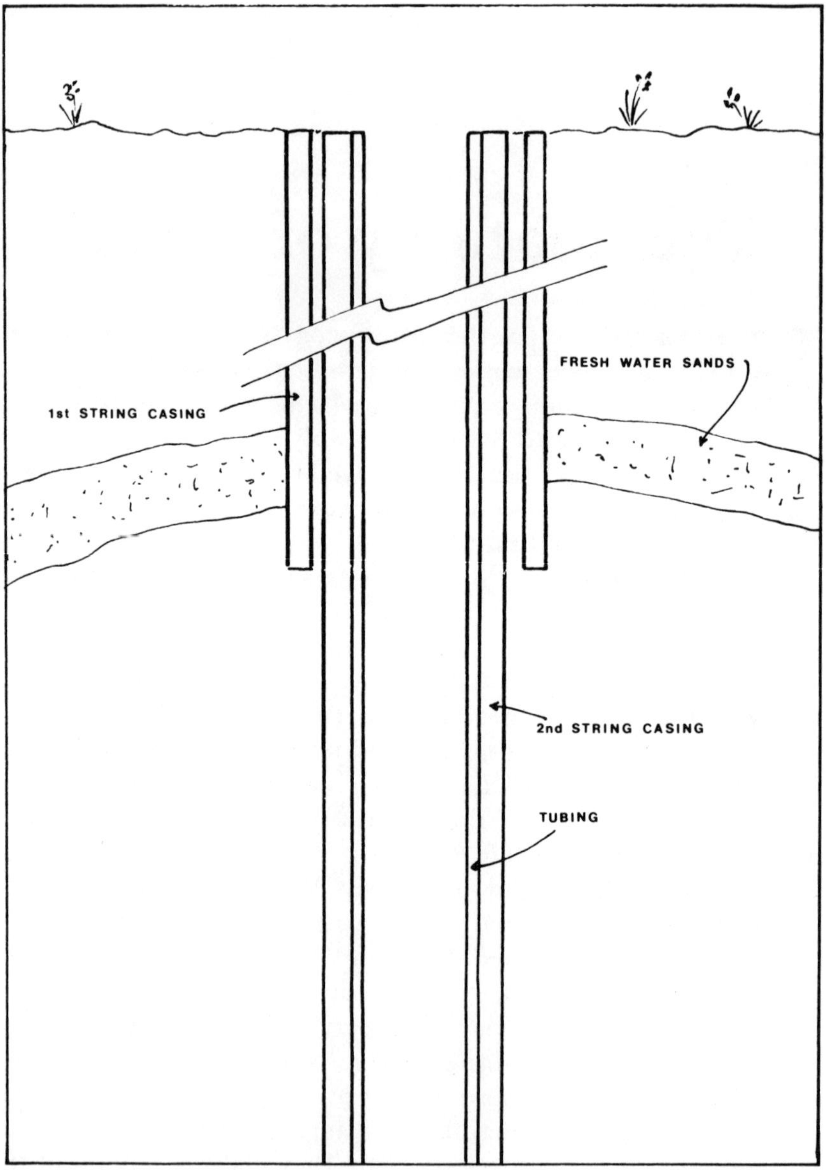

The upper portion of the hole must be designed to provide protection for the subsurface fresh water.

The maximum depth of a well is not something that the operator decides by a flip of the coin or something that he can vary depending on how much money he's got left. Before drilling is started, he must apply for a permit. At that time, he is required to state the expected maximum depth of the well. Once the permit has been issued, he can go to that depth and no farther. Obviously, if a meaningful pool of oil is found before he gets to the permissible depth, he can stop drilling. But if he wants to go down deeper, he will have to apply for a new permit to a new prestated depth. Despite all of the available geological science and technique, much of this is guesswork, based on known or suspected geological formations of the subterranean strata, the known depth of previously discovered oil reserves in that general area, or simply wishful thinking. Nobody knows for sure where there is oil until someone drills a hole and finds it. While there is no hard and fast rule, most wells drilled by independent operators in the U.S. tend to average between 4,000 and 8,000 feet, meaning that the cost of completing a well can average between $120,000 and $250,000.

No drilling activity can commence without a ready supply of ample amounts of water. Thus, once the derrick is erected, arrangements must be made to pipe water to the rig. Only then can drilling commence. The first hundred or so feet of the hole must be designed to provide protection for the subsurface fresh water which is used for drinking and irrigation by anyone living in the vicinity. If this were not done, fluids and salt water dredged from greater depths might seep into the fresh-water sands, polluting the water supply. To achieve this, the first part of the hole is of a greater diameter, usually about one foot. Into this, surface or protection pipe is lowered and cemented in place, providing a nonporous wall.

Once this has been accomplished, the main drilling operation can proceed, usually using a seven- to nine-inch diameter bit. As a general rule, these bits are made of case-hardened steel and consist of two or three rotating cones covered with sharp teeth which crush then grind rock or other solid matter into small fragments. Oversimplified, the drill bit is attached to lengths of hollow drillpipe which are rotated by surface machinery. But in order to function properly there must be lubrication and a means of bringing the ground-up rock debris up to the surface. That is the function of the drilling mud.

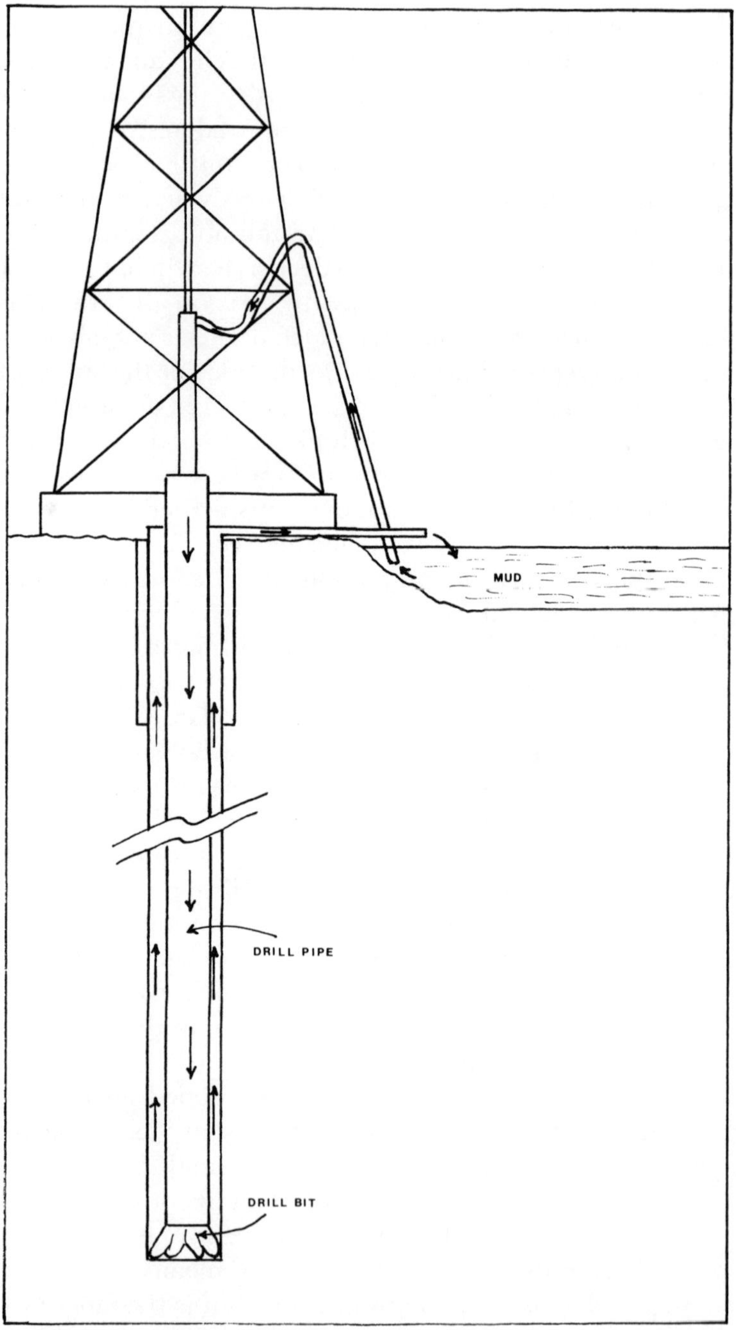

The mud is mixed in a shallow mud pit next to the well and pumped down through the center of the drillpipe and out through the drill bit. The pressure is sufficient to force it to return to the surface on the outside of the drillpipe and back into the mud pit.

It may seem depressing to think in terms of thousands, often tens of thousands of dollars spent for mud, but without it the entire operation would be impossible. Though it is simply called mud, it actually is a chemical mixture prepared in a shallow pit next to the well and pumped down through the center of the drillpipe and out through the drill bit. The pressure forces it to return to the surface on the outside of the drillpipe and back into the mud pit. Thus, the mud lubricates the drillpipe and drill bit, brings debris out of the hole and up to the surface, and helps prevent the walls of the hole from caving in.

But once the preplanned depth has been reached, don't expect to have oil (or gas) pour out of it. Likewise don't assume the hole is dry because it isn't a gusher. What happens next to determine the presence of oil is a process called logging the well. This means every known technique is employed, usually by a service company which specializes in such work, to determine if any of the various layers of subsurface strata show indications of the presence of oil.

In practice, logging consists of lowering a variety of electrical instruments into the hole and recording impulses received by these instruments on a graph. A trained geologist can then read that graph and make an educated guess as to the likelihood of the presence of oil or gas in any one or several of these strata. In the event that one or several particular formations look promising, a core gun is sometimes lowered into the hole. It fires small charges into these formations, obtaining core samples which can be examined by experts. When such an examination proves favorable, the well will probably turn out to be a producer. For how long, nobody can predict.

But even now we're only halfway home. Now that it has been determined that there is oil, the next step is to get the well into production. (Free-flowing wells, or gushers, are so rare that we don't need to concern ourselves with them.) Again, specialized service companies are employed to supply the talent, equipment, and tools to complete the well. The first part of this job is to install smaller-diameter casing, similar to that which was used to protect the fresh-water supply, all the way down to the bottom of the well (downhole). It prevents the well walls from collapsing and seals out any of the salt water which tends to be found in great quantities at the lower depths. The casing is a permanent installation and must

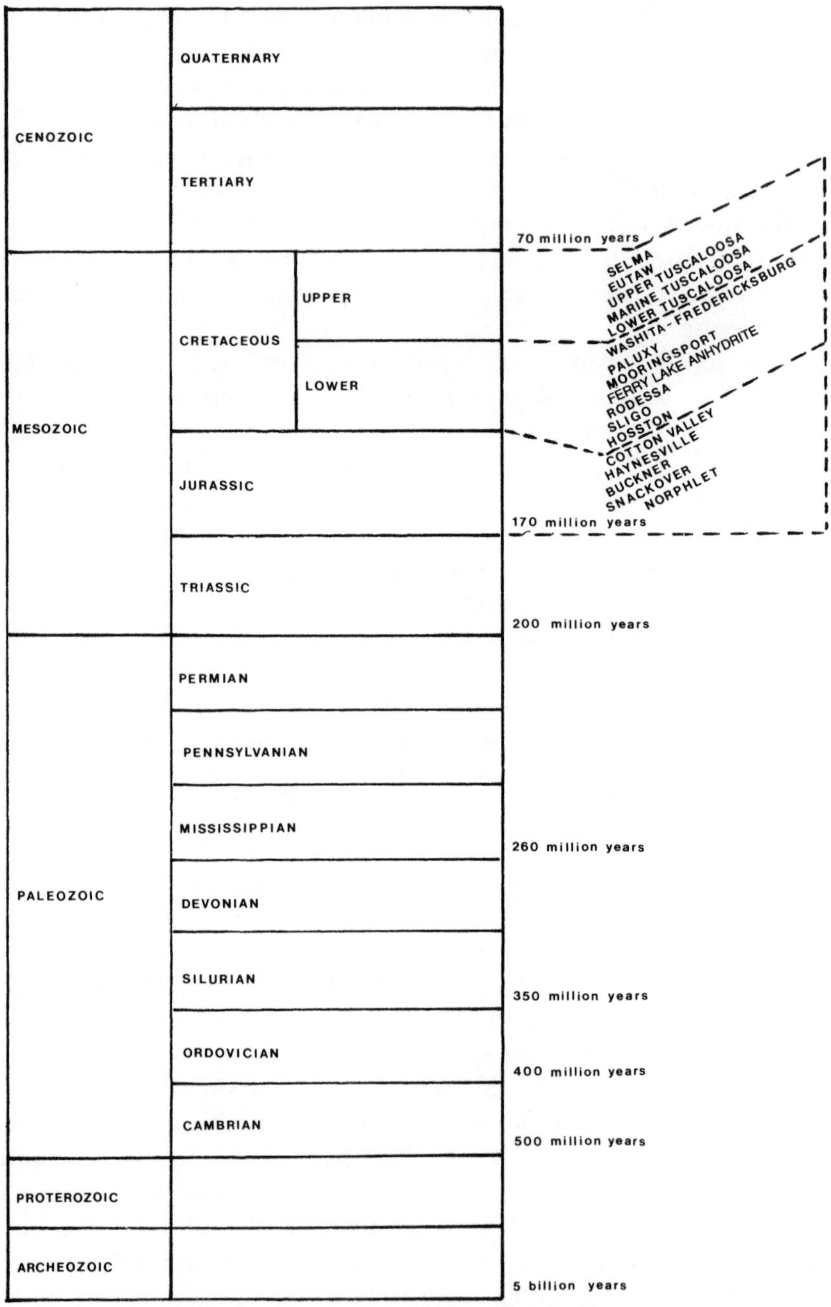

The subsurface strata which are most often referred to with reference to oil and gas exploration.

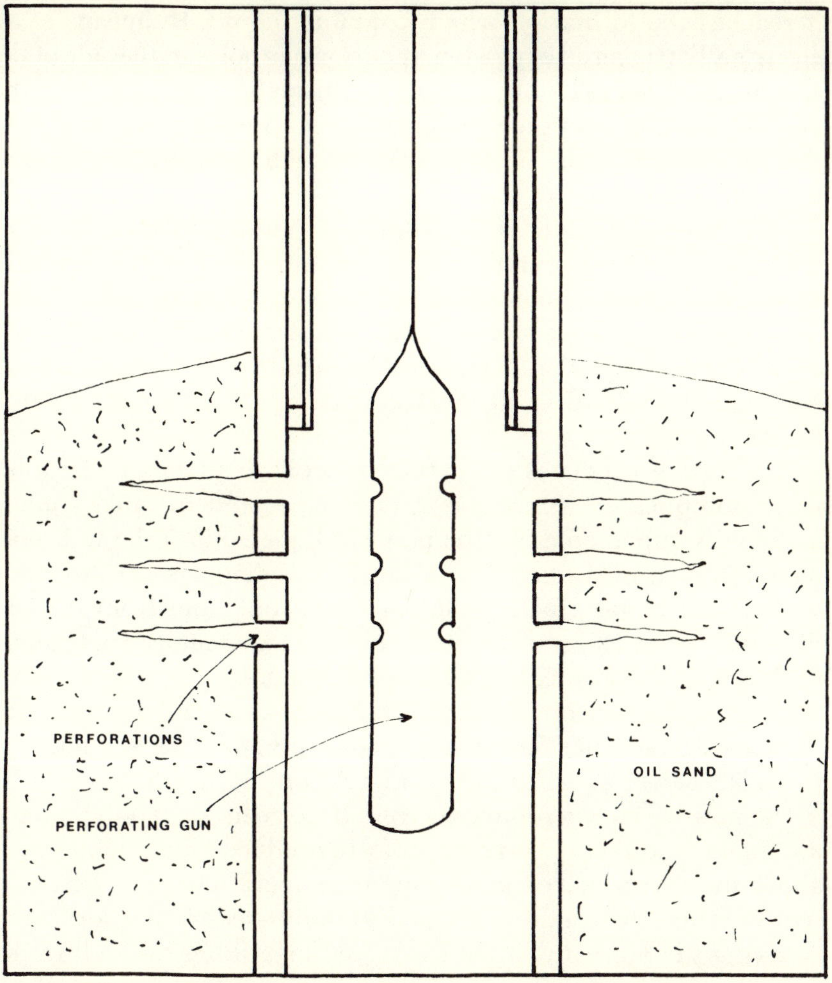

A perforation gun is lowered into the hole until it reaches the formation which contains the oil. By means of an electrically triggered explosion, it perforates the side of the casing and liner.

be protected from wear. This is accomplished by installing a temporary, removable liner which absorbs the wear and tear associated with pumping the oil out of the ground. It must be replaced periodically to continue providing adequate protection for the casing.

We now have an airtight, watertight pipe going down into the ground for thousands of feet. The next problem is to get the oil into that pipe. To do this, a perforation gun is lowered into the hole until it reaches the formation which contains the oil. By means of an electrically triggered explosion, it perforates holes in the side of the casing and liner. The oil then seeps through these holes into the well. If the oil formation is under sufficient pressure, it may flow to the surface by itself. If there isn't enough pressure, a pump is installed to improve flow.

All that is left now is to install the pump and the necessary machinery to keep it pumping (or, in the case of a free-flowing well, a system of pressure-controlling pipes and valves called a Christmas tree) and either a storage tank to collect the oil for pickup by oil-company trucks or a pipeline connecting the wellhead with storage terminals. After all, you can't market oil if you can't get it to the marketplace.

If the well produces gas rather than oil, this tends to get a bit more complicated. Since gas cannot be stored in tanks (unless artificially supercooled to the point of liquefaction) the well may have to be capped temporarily until arrangements can be made with a natural-gas pipeline company to install a line from the well directly to one of its collection points. Occasionally this causes problems if the well is a remote, low-producer.

Some wells turn out to be simultaneous gas and oil producers. In these cases, facilities for oil storage and pipelines for gas must be provided before actual production can commence.

So now we have a producing well. If we're lucky, it will produce a sufficient number of barrels per day to produce a reasonable profit above the cost involved in keeping it in operation. Even better, it will continue to produce at a reasonably steady rate for years, repaying the huge investment involved in drilling the well in the first place and returning a continuing profit for all concerned.

3

The good old days and the better new days

Typical of the wild and woolly days of early oil exploration was what happened in East Texas in the mid-1920s. Columbus Marion Joiner, known to his friends as "Dad" Joiner, arrived in Rusk County, East Texas, where more than a dozen exploratory dry holes had already been drilled. Convinced that there was oil to be found and apparently being a persuasive fellow, he insisted to all who would listen that he was sitting on top of a veritable ocean of oil. Many agreed to lease their land to him for no more than the assurance that he would drill a well and that the payoff would come as soon as oil was found. One of those persuaded was Daisy Bradford, and in August 1927 Dad Joiner went to work near a creek on her farm.

The equipment he assembled would make the oilmen of today throw up their hands in horror. It consisted of a derrick made of pine lumber, a cotton-gin boiler for power, and a bunch of rusted and slightly twisted pipe. His crew was not much better. They were mostly farmhands with only one experienced driller to tell them what to do and how to do it. This first well, the Daisy Bradford No. 1, was drilled to a depth of 1,098 feet. Upon reaching that depth, a section of the pipe became stuck in the hole and the well had to be abandoned.

The next attempt was made about 100 feet from the first. This time, the crew got all the way to 2,518 feet before the drill bit twisted off and could not be retrieved. Again, the attempt had to be abandoned. By now, the better part of a year had passed and so had Dad Joiner's 70th birthday. Stooped by age, financially broke, but still able to use his powers of persuasion with a degree of success, he once more set out to raise additional funds. This time, he convinced Ed Laster, a skilled and experienced driller, to take charge of the drilling operation. Laster nearly quit when he saw the pile of junk that Joiner called his drilling equipment, but somehow the challenge seemed to fascinate him and he stayed on.

The site which offered the greatest promise was about 400 feet from the second hole. But somehow, during the attempt at moving the derrick and equipment from the old location to the new one, it got stuck about 100 feet short of its destination. Well, 100 feet didn't seem that important. "We'll drill right here," Joiner told Laster and the crew. Thus, Daisy Bradford No. 3 was spudded-in in May 1929.

But all kinds of problems continued to haunt their attempt. The boiler, fired with cord wood and old automobile tires, cracked and had to be replaced with another liberated from a sawmill. Money, too, was running short, and Joiner found that his abilities to raise more were hampered by the opinions of fellow oilmen who considered him a fast-talking promoter whose chances of success were less than nil. Worse, when cores taken at just below 3,400 feet showed traces of oil, Joiner was accused of salting the cores (planting oil in the sand which made up the cores) to convince investors to part with their money.

The day was September 3, 1930. News had leaked out that a drillstem test would be made, and farmers, oil scouts, and businessmen streamed to the Bradford farm. It was late afternoon when the Daisy Bradford No. 3 started to shudder and tremble. Quite suddenly, a stream of oil, water, and mud shot up into the derrick. Excitement gripped everyone present, and even the conservative Ed Laster had to admit that the prospects looked favorable.

It took another month to complete the well, and the final casings were put down during the night of October 2. By the next day, a crowd of close to 10,000 people had gathered. But again, nothing happened. More tests were made, but no oil was produced. Then, after dark on Sunday, October 5, when Laster and his crew were working by lanternlight, a muffled roar was heard. "Put out the fires!" Just as the last of the lanterns had been extinguished, a stream of oil and water shot up with a deafening roar, falling like rain on everyone around. It stopped and started again in spurts, eventually flowing at a rate of 100 barrels in 20 minutes.

By the standards of those days, when oil was selling at around $1 a barrel, the Daisy Bradford No. 3 was never a large producer, eventually yielding an average of 400 barrels per day. By contrast, on December 28, 1930, a well drilled nine miles to the north came in with a bang, producing 22,000 barrels of oil per day. Be that as it may, it was the Joiner well which proved the presence of oil in East Texas, an area which subsequently attracted thousands who drilled over 26,000 producing wells, making the area for some time to come the largest oil-producing field in North America.

This sudden glut of oil at a time when energy needs were small by today's standards produced such a surplus that the price per barrel soon fell to below fifteen cents. Some type of regulation was obviously needed because the economy simply couldn't absorb the 400,000-plus barrels which were flowing daily from that one field alone, but it took until November 1932 when the Texas legislature passed a bill that placed the control of oil production under the supervision of the Texas Railroad Commission. This legislation, which is still in force today, returned a degree of sanity to the oil business and, as a result, crude oil prices slowly began to rise again. This so-called proration is the conservation measure which has since been adopted everywhere in order to protect fields from over-production and the resulting loss of pressure that might eventually have destroyed them. Even today, estimates are that the East Texas Field alone still contains over two billion barrels of recoverable oil.

Yes, things have changed a lot since Dad Joiner's time. One of the most important changes involves the improvements in drilling techniques and the ways in which we have learned to improve the productivity of marginal oil and gas wells. The other change, at least equal in importance, is the huge increase in the price being paid for crude oil and natural gas. Less than a decade ago, before OPEC (the oil-producing countries from whom the U.S. receives about 85% of its imported oil) decided to exert its power, a barrel of crude oil sold for $3 to $5. In the intervening years, this price has risen tenfold, in turn increasing the price for domestic oil by a comparable margin. The unfavorable result of this has been the increase in the prices of gasoline, heating oil, and virtually all commodities which use petroleum in their production. Indirectly, it has resulted in vastly accelerated inflation because there is hardly anything we buy or do in our lives these days that doesn't depend to a considerable degree on fuel-consuming transportation.

But there is also a positive side to all of this. Because of the increase in the price paid for oil and gas, wells which used to be considered marginal or wholly unprofitable can now be operated at a profit. As a result, large numbers of these older wells are either being reopened or redrilled. In addition, there continues to be a huge upswing in the activity revolving around the search for new oil and gas, both in areas which contain proven reserves and in areas without a past history of energy production. As a matter of fact, despite the imposition of punitive "windfall" profits taxes, the exploration activity has increased to where developers are, on occasion, faced with a shortage of drilling equipment and materials. In fact it has increased to where 64,306 wells were drilled and completed in 1980 alone.

All of this new drilling activity falls into three basic categories. The one which has attracted the most attention from the press and is therefore best-known to the public is the effort to extract oil and gas from hard-to-work locations such as offshore in the Gulf of Mexico, on the Alaskan North Slope, in the Prudhoe Bay area, off the Atlantic and Pacific Coasts, and in the North Sea. Virtually all of this work is being done by major oil companies, often by consortiums consisting of several such major companies because the necessary risk-capital investment is too large to be handled by independent entrepreneurs. To them, a small investment is $1 million. They prefer to go to banks where loans of any size are available. The only way the average investor can participate is to buy stock.

Two other categories have attracted comparatively little attention. They involve exploration activities in areas of known oil and gas reserves, such as the East Texas Field, the Permian Basin in West Texas and eastern New Mexico, the known oil fields in Pennsylvania, Oklahoma, Kansas, and California, plus wildcat activities being conducted just about anywhere geologists believe there is even the slightest possiblity of success. Two of the most exciting of these new areas are the Williston Basin and the Overthrust Belt in the Rockies, extending along the Continental Divide from Canada to Mexico.

Success stories such as Dad Joiner's have lured investors and entrepreneurs throughout the ensuing decades to this business of

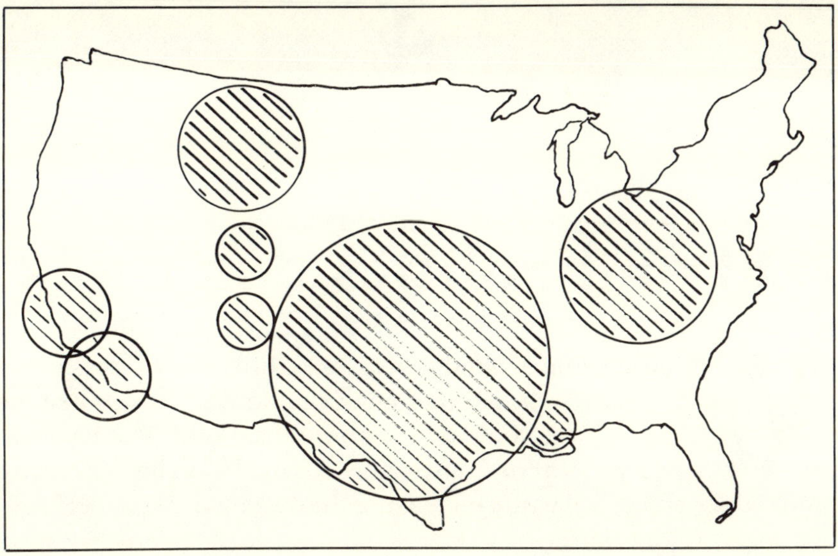

Approximate areas in the U.S. which have produced meaningful quantities of oil and natural gas.

drilling for oil and natural gas. Many made fortunes for themselves, their partners, their friends, and investors. Others lost their shirts. Even today, not a great deal has changed. Granted, few people envision new discoveries of the magnitude of the East Texas Field or that of the famous Permian Basin. But with newly discovered oil selling for between $30–$40 a barrel, marginal wells—which in years past might have been capped as not worthwhile—are now considered commercially profitable. Many wells, even those producing as little as two or three barrels per day, can eventually pay off the initial investment and even return a profit to all involved.

Today, by far the largest amount of U.S. speculative drilling is being undertaken by independent entrepreneurs, often individuals or small groups which are financed by private capital. By investing in the efforts of these individuals, the average person with a limited amount of risk capital can participate in the profit potential associated with oil and gas—an industry which has never looked better.

4

Oil and politics don't mix

When driving around places like Midland or Odessa, you find cars with bumper stickers reading, "If you like the Post Office, you'll love nationalized oil." The implication is that, as a general rule, government can always foul things up and reduce efficiency while increasing the cost involved in performing a given function.

Since its inception, the petroleum industry has done a poor job in terms of public relations. As a result, the public believes all oilmen are robber barons concerned exclusively with milking the people. And, in the past, there was a degree of justification for this impression. However, no individual or company would willingly expend the huge amounts of risk capital involved in exploration, production, transportation, and refining unless there were a potential for sufficiently large profits to offset the possibility—in fact, probability—of incurring losses of immense proportions.

Largely because of this negative public image, coupled with the awareness that energy production is the lifeblood of this country, politicians have recently found it advantageous to impose regulations and restrictions on the oil companies to imply they are protecting the "little people." The result is that the pricing restriction placed on domestic oil made exploration uneconomical. More profit could be obtained at much less risk by going into partnership with foreign governments and by importing this foreign oil despite the extra expense of long-distance transportation. Before we knew it, a huge percentage of the oil which makes this country function had its origin in some far-off Arab sheikdom.

Then came the rude awakening. The Arabs, angry with our pro-Israeli policies and aware that they had us backed into a corner, formed OPEC and raised the price of their crude oil by several thousand percent. And this country, characteristically slow to react with politically "unpopular" steps, made the average consumer a subsidizer of Arabian wealth. It took several additional years for the Administration to get enough courage to propose a degree of deregulation of the oil industry, something which, if it had happened before the OPEC boycott, might have been instrumental in minimizing the dependence of the U.S. on imported oil and thus the whims of relatively unreliable foreign governments.

Today, the media are conveying stories which would have us believe that the energy reserves in this country, excluding coal, are insufficient to fill our needs now or in the future. The fact is that nobody actually knows. There is a lot of talk of "proven reserves," but nobody has been down there below the ground to measure them. Among leading geologists, the consensus is that there is a total of 3 million square miles of potentially oil- or gas-producing areas in the U.S., and only two percent have been drilled to any meaningful extent. Granted, nobody is expecting to find producing giants such as the Yates Field in Texas which has given 25,000 barrels per day for the last 50 years, and which is expected to continue at that rate for another 50–100 years. But small wells also produce oil. A thousand wells producing two barrels a day are as good as one which produces 2,000 barrels. With the public favoring energy self-sufficiency and less government intervention, we may actually reduce our dependence on foreign oil by a considerable margin.

Another political confrontation has been the environment. In recent years, the urge to protect the environment has become a major preoccupation of government agencies and the rallying cry of a score of organizations in the private sector. Just as the earlier disregard for the environment resulted in serious abuses, so is this new concern bringing about excesses in terms of protective regulations which frequently go too far.

One of the favorite claims is that the environment is fragile and any damage done to it is irreversible. Granted, man has done damage to the environment and continues to do so. But so does nature with its floods, volcanoes, and earthquakes. Yet, time and time again, nature responds with great resilience and repairs itself as soon as the disturbance is removed. Oil spills have killed wildlife and temporarily fouled the land, but considering its need in daily life, its detrimental effect is no greater than empty beer cans and garbage by the side of the road.

Excessive concern for the environment has a detrimental if not disastrous effect on this country's energy dependence. It has caused costly delays and occasional cancellations of major exploration activities when our dependence on foreign oil is putting us in an increasingly precarious position. It is a crime that a country of the size and resources of the U.S. must cater to the whims of unstable governments of a collection of small, relatively unreliable countries.

We must learn to become realists and accept that this country's primary objective for the next decade or two is achieving complete and uncompromised energy independence. No avenue toward that goal can be left unexplored. The discovery of new oil is still the fastest and easiest method of at least reducing our dependence on the OPEC countries.

There can be no doubt that alternative sources of energy will be playing an increasingly important part, gradually replacing ever-greater amounts of oil and natural gas. There is coal which is in ample supply, but which is not likely to find its way into our automobile engines. There is nuclear energy which will play an increasingly important role, but which isn't a practical substitute for gasoline. Then there is solar energy, which is bound to play an increasingly important part in terms of generating clean, unending heat and electricity.

Even if the need for oil in all forms of energy production would suddenly cease, and that is extremely unlikely, the need for huge amounts of petroleum would still exist. As a general rule, we think of oil as gasoline, diesel and jet fuel, kerosene, and lubricants. We tend to forget the long and constantly growing list of products of the petrochemical industry which uses petroleum in the manufacture of practically everything we use daily: fertilizers, pesticides, fungicides; paints, pigments, waxes, thinners, solvents, cleaning fluids, detergents; refrigerants and antifreeze; resins, adhesives, sealants, insulation; latex, rubber compounds, all manner of plastics, films; substitutes for glass, leather, wood, bone, metal and fabrics; synthetic fibers; medicines, cosmetics; toys and tools. If every item containing petroleum were suddenly removed from your home or office, you'd be standing in a bare, unpainted room.

We all know that fossil fuels, oil and natural gas, are not going to last forever. Someday, probably toward the end of the 21st century, the last drop of oil will be squeezed from the last insignificant oil-bearing formation. But that's one hundred years in the future. In the interim, we must encourage ever-increasing exploration of whatever is still available in terms of energy sources in the bowels of the earth.

Hardly a day goes by without some new development, application, material, product which is the result of one more chemical derivative of oil. This trend is bound to continue more or less indefinitely and the worldwide market for petroleum-based products can be expected to grow continually for decades if politics stays out of petroleum.

In the future, the value of a barrel of oil and, in turn, the price paid for it will increase as its use for the purpose of energy production decreases. Thus, oil will be needed for at least as long as our lifetime. In turn, an investment in a producing well with ample reserves will pay handsomely for an indefinite period of time.

5

Who owns all that oil and gas?

With new oil and gas discoveries being made with increasing frequency in areas where exploration activities were nil, the question of ownership becomes important. You just don't go up to the local farmer and shake hands on a deal. Technically, the person, organization, company, or government which owns a piece of real estate, no matter its size, also owns the rights to whatever minerals may be hidden below that piece of real estate. In practice, however, this is rarely true. In many sections of the country, residential property may exclude mineral rights. The deed probably won't state who does own the mineral rights, but in all likelihood you wouldn't care.

Oddly enough, the U.S. is the only country in the world where the government does not own all mineral rights. Persons who own farms, ranches, or tracts of land at some distance from densely populated areas in most cases buy the mineral rights under that land at the time of purchase. But mineral rights can be sold without affecting surface rights. Thus, a farmer with a succession of bad years may sell the mineral rights under part or all of his land. In fact, the owner of a tract of land often sells the mineral rights down to a certain depth to one buyer and the mineral rights for depths below that limit to another. A subsequent buyer who wants to acquire that farm will only be able to buy the surface rights from the farmer, either foregoing ownership of the mineral rights or offering to buy them back.

What this means to the company or person interested in drilling an exploratory well on the property is that he must negotiate the lease with both the owner of the surface rights and the various

don't lease
BUY

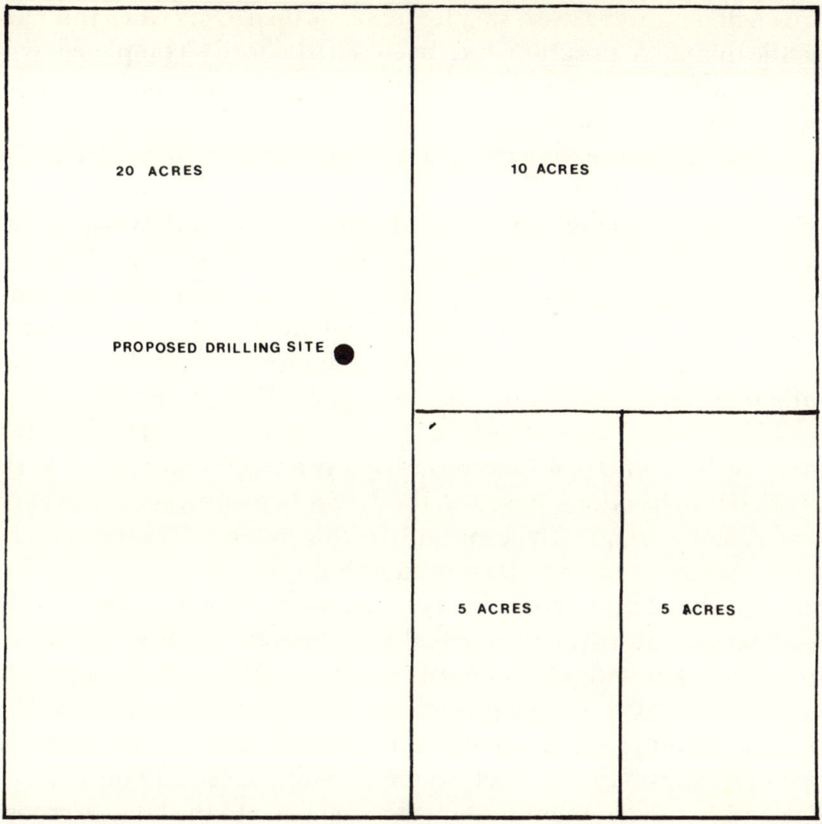

The average drilling unit consists of 40 acres which may be owned by different individuals and the mineral rights which may be owned by different additional persons.

owners of the mineral rights. But that isn't all. Since it would be foolish to spend the money to drill an exploratory well without having the right to drill additional wells on adjacent property in the event that the initial wildcat is successful, the average single drilling unit usually involves a minimum of 40 acres. More frequently, leases will be acquired for several such units adjacent to each other to ensure the opportunity to develop the field fully.

Acquiring the necessary leases for such an operation may involve contacting hundreds of individuals all over the country, each of whom has a fractional interest in the surface or mineral rights. Normally, the individual or company planning to drill in a certain area will obtain the necessary leases on its own. Only when this part of the planned program has been satisfactorily completed will potential investors be contacted to collect the necessary funds to undertake the actual drilling.

An oil or gas lease is a fairly standard contract which calls for the payment of a royalty, usually 12.5 percent or more, to the lessors (the persons owning the various rights), in case oil or gas is discovered, plus a bonus—a rental fee of so much per acre. This fee, which may range from $1–$2 per acre to several times that amount, gives the operator one year in which to drill his well. If more time is needed, additional delay-rental fees must be paid annually, although they are usually only a fraction of the initial bonus.

Obviously, if several lessors are involved in a single lease for a given drilling unit of 40 acres, the royalty as well as the rental fee is divided into fractions, based on the percentage of ownership of each lessor. Not infrequently, especially if the area is near other known oil or gas reserves, the lessors may hold out for more than that one-eighth (12.5 percent) royalty, and the operator may find that he has to agree to an overriding royalty, the amount of which is subject to negotiation with all involved.

In all of this, a person owning only the surface and not the mineral rights is left out in the cold. The best he can expect from the operator is a small fee in return for providing access to the drilling site and reimbursement for any damage done to the land or crops.

In view of the mammoth increase in exploration activity in all parts of the country, landowners as individuals or in groups may actually wish to set up a consortium into which they pool all the mineral rights for a given area to offer to an oil company or independent operator; or they may hire a drilling contractor themselves. In the first instance, the operator puts together the necessary funds to conduct the actual drilling operation, although any one of the individuals or the consortium as a whole may participate in the financing. In the second instance, the landowner group must provide the entire financing.

In addition to individually owned lands, there are millions of acres in the U.S. which are owned and operated by the government. At regular intervals, the Bureau of Land Management will offer mineral leases to the public at relatively low cost. These offers, along with the rules governing them, are periodically published by the government and anyone interested can enter a bid. But the simple acquisition of the mineral rights to a tract of government land does not necessarily mean that there is someone waiting to drill a hole. An interested operator must be found within a given period of time; if no exploration takes place, the rights revert back to the government.

A little-known fact is that many major oil companies hold large mineral leases within the continental U.S.—leases which they are often unwilling or unable to exploit because of the immense scope of their offshore and overseas activities. Often, they let independents drill on these leases under some type of percentage arrangement. Referred to as oil-corporation farm-outs, they usually call for a division of the net revenues under which the independent operator, along with his investors, pays for all costs associated with drilling and retains from 60–75 percent of the net returns.

By far the largest amount of oil and gas discovered in this country (onshore) was drilled for and found by independent operators rather than the majors. Their primary activity relative to onshore oil is restricted to refining and marketing. Offshore activities promise to produce the largest remaining returns in terms of discoverable reserves—activities beyond the reach of the average investor.

6

The mathematics of investment

Investing in oil is a gamble. But any gambler worth his weight in salt will compare the odds against other forms of gambling. If not oil, what else? In roulette, dice, and blackjack, the odds are at least thirty to one against you, and then you have to deal with the Internal Revenue Service even before you leave the cashier's window. In addition, tax laws permit writing off gambling losses only to the extent of gambling winnings, while winnings are taxed without limit. In short, anyone using risk money in the hopes of respectable gain by placing it on the gaming table has every conceivable strike against him. At the horse races, playing favorites may return anywhere from two to five to one which, considering the equally good chance of losing the investment, seems like poor odds. Blue chip stocks are comfortable, but "glamour" stocks fluctuate greatly in value, and just one wrong word said by a White House official can cause them to plummet. In addition, there are broker's fees, taxes on dividends, and the fact that the actual cash return on the investment is small unless you sell at precisely the right moment.

There is simply no other form of investment which can compare with oil and natural gas. The chance of loss is common to all, although it may be greater in the oil and gas business, but the potential return when things work out is so superior that it more than offsets the added risk. As a general rule, people like to say that the chances of having a meaningful oil or gas strike are nine to one. In fact, the chance of coming up with a moderate but continuing return on an investment in an area of known reserves is probably more like three to one, while the odds of a successful wildcat operation are twenty-five to one. However, in these cases the payoff is vastly greater.

The lure of investing in oil or gas exploration is largely based on two elements: the possibility, though slight, of making a real killing and the fact that the original investment can be written off against taxes in the year when the investment is made, reducing the risk to the amount not covered by the reduction in the amount of taxes owed. But how great is that reduction? It depends entirely on your tax bracket—the percentage of taxes you must pay relative to your adjusted gross income.

Say you have $5,000 in a savings account earning 5–10 percent annually, meaning you lose between 12–18 percent per year from the current inflation rate. You figure you might as well invest in a risk situation where there is at least a chance, though slim, of making a decent profit. Assuming the drilling project which you have selected ends up in a dry hole and the entire amount is lost, how much of a loss in terms of dollars and cents do you actually incur?

If your adjusted gross income after deducting the $5,000 investment amounts to $250,000 (in which case you'll undoubtedly have an accountant figure all this out), your tax will be $141,724.00 or 56.7 percent of your adjusted gross income (1979 tax rates). This means that the amount of the $5,000 investment lost amounts to $2,165, while the remaining $2,835 are amortized in terms of a tax break. If your adjusted gross income after deducting the investment amounts to $100,000, the tax would be $41,998.00 or 42 percent of the adjusted gross income. This means that the actual loss from the $5,000 investment would be $2,900.10, with $2,099.90 as a tax break. If your adjusted gross income is only $25,000, then your tax would be $4,633 or 18.5 percent. In this case, the tax reduction would take care of only $926.60 of the investment loss; $4073.40 would be the actual loss.

This reasoning has caused many drilling funds to make a rule not to accept investments from individuals who are below the 50-percent tax bracket. Still, if you're willing to take a chance and you want to participate in one of these restrictive funds, you can always lie. If you end up with a total loss, you have only yourself to blame.

In contrast to the large SEC-registered drilling funds, the small, private funds rarely have prerequisites for submitting a financial statement. They should and usually do tell you in advance that there is a better-than-even chance that your investment will either be lost or never produce a meaningful profit. Then if you decide to risk your money, it's your decision.

The whole point of this exercise in mathematics is to point out that tax shelters are available only to those who have sufficiently large incomes—over the 50 percent bracket. One exception to this is if you're self-employed and your gross income is $40,000. If you've made a lot of legitimate business expenses, say $32,000, your adjusted gross income would be $8,000. During this same year, you deducted $5,000 from your savings account and invested it in a drilling venture. This will leave your adjusted gross income at $3,000, resulting in a zero tax payment (1979 tax figures). Taxes for the $8,000 would have been $378, meaning the amount risked is $4,622. But since a zero tax on a $40,000 gross income looks suspicious, you may have quite a bit of explaining to do when you're audited. Thus, it might be better to take only some of the deductions this year and defer the rest to future years. Then you'll pay at least a small amount of tax and reduce the risk of an audit.

Anyone faced with a marginal tax situation should consult a knowledgable accountant. Our tax laws are too complicated and convoluted, not to mention the ridiculously obscure language they are written in, for the average layman to decipher. Don't take needless risks on an already risky venture by trying to do your accounting yourself.

If you aren't over the 50-percent bracket, where can you come up with the available cash for an investment? Unbelievable as it may seem, nearly every person with a moderate income can have enough money within two years for a sizeable investment.

First, you must understand the difference between discretionary funds and risk capital. Discretionary funds are spent for luxuries or nonessential commodities. Practically every day we spend in addition to what is necessary a certain amount for luxuries to gratify our desires of the moment. There are no statistics, but probably 20 percent of a person's payouts are the actual or marginal luxuries—convenience items.

Risk capital is what is left over after all essential and luxury items have been bought. Intelligent use of risk capital can make a person financially independent for his lifetime, but accumulating it isn't easy unless he's in the 50-percent tax bracket. At least, most people don't seem to be able to set money aside for potentially profitable speculation. But to be completely honest, this isn't really true. Anyone whose income today (1981) is over $30,000 could easily accumulate a $5,000 risk capital fund by simply limiting his discretionary funds. Life might be a bit less flamboyant, but that $5,000 or $10,000 saved in a year or two might represent your price of admission to financial independence.

7

How to find, evaluate, and identify investment opportunities

Anyone confronted for the first time with the problem of locating investment opportunities in the oil and gas industry may not know where to turn. There isn't exactly an 800-number to call and ask who needs money to drill a well, and there is no hard and fast rule or central agency to steer the potential investor in the right direction.

Depending on the type of investment which interests you, there are a number of different avenues to follow. If you're interested in participating in one of the major drilling funds, the solution to the problem is relatively simple. Most stockbrokers will know of one or several such funds which are currently putting together the financing for another exploration program. But don't accept the first offer that comes along. Ask for and examine all printed material about the offering and the company making it. How long has this company been in business? What have been the results in terms of returns to the limited partners? What has been its past drilling activity?

As in virtually any field, there are a few shady characters here and there in the oil business. Happily, they are the exception rather than the rule, but certain individual operators and some rather sizable drilling funds have attracted investments without ever actually spending all or even most of this investment in speculative drilling operations. Instead, much of the money disappears into thin air, used for "overhead": huge salaries for corporate executives, outfitting excessively fancy offices, purchasing entire office buildings, extensive advertising and promotions, and other activities which bring no return to the investor.

The only sure way to be certain a given operator will use your investment money wisely is to check into his past performance carefully. This does not necessarily mean that an operator who has drilled several dry holes should be avoided. As a general rule, eight out of nine drilling projects result in dry holes, so someone with a record of a dozen dry holes might hit it big next time. It is the amount of actual drilling activity relative to the amount of investment in each instance that should be the criterion.

There are a number of ways to check on the reputation of an operator or a drilling fund. One is to make inquiries at one or several banks in the headquarters town of the operator. While actual financial information may be confidential and, therefore, not readily available, good bankers will steer a potential investor away from a questionable prospect. If that doesn't work, visit the offices of the nearest Independent Oil Producers' Association (Appendix). A third possibility would be to have your accountant or attorney do some checking. Or you may wish to contact previous investors. Their experience should indicate the operator's performance record.

There are always companies which make the lion's share of their profits by charging exorbitant management fees, while keeping their drilling activity to a minimum. Obviously, such a company is a poor investment. Even if the company itself checks out, you may wish to know where the tracts are, what percentage of the proposed drilling activity will take place in areas of proven reserves, and which percentage will involve highly speculative wildcatting. In other words, taking your time and doing careful research may increase your chances of eventual profit considerably.

If you're looking for an opportunity to make a small or medium-sized investment in one of the independent operations which are too small to require registration with the SEC, the problem of finding the right individual or group becomes much more complicated. Where there is a fair amount of oil or gas exploration activity, one can usually find banks in which one executive or possibly even an entire department deals in financial matters related to oil. Frequently, these people may suggest the names of some operators whom they consider reliable. CPAs are also good sources for such information.

Another source might be to look in the Yellow Pages under "Oil and Gas Exploration and Development," "Oil Operators," or "Oil Producers." Another heading is "Geologists." As a general rule, those people involved in the oil business are friendly, gregarious, and approachable, and a few phone calls should produce at least one person who can make a contact. Other names will come from that one, and pretty soon you'll have contacted a half dozen people who, in one way or another, may steer you in the right direction.

When you're actually ready to approach an independent operator with the suggestion that you might be willing to invest some money in a future drilling program, be sure to pay close attention to his reaction. The first thing he should tell you is that the risk is considerable and that there is a good chance you'll be losing your investment. If, instead, he implies that the chances are even or better that you'll be making a lot of money, watch out. While independents as a group are honest, trustworthy individuals, there are hotshots and crooks in every business. Always look into the past history of the operator you have selected. Make sure that he has consistently used investment money for actual drilling operations, and that at least some of these have been profitable.

Another suggestion would be to contact one of the many oil and gas associations, the names of which can also be found in the Yellow Pages of most major cities and state capitals and in the Appendix of this book. In most instances, these people will know who is active where and who has had a good record in terms of past performance.

If none of this is practical in your city or town, it might be worthwhile to travel to Midland or Odessa, Texas. These cities virtually float on oil, and there is hardly anyone who isn't involved in the oil business in one way or another or at least knows someone who is. Again, just one initial contact is bound to snowball into dozens. One of the advantages of such a visit would be the opportunity to learn about the business. Even though you may have no intention of ever becoming actively involved in it, the more you know and understand how it works, what is involved, and why exploration is as expensive and speculative as it is, the better will be your chance to use your risk money intelligently, minimizing the chances of total loss.

The best advice for the first-time investor is take your time. Don't get impatient and jump in with both feet. Do as much research as possible—the more the better. Like all specialized businesses, the oil industry is full of terms and phrases which are meaningless to the uninitiated. Find out what they mean, so when someone starts throwing them around you'll at least have a vague idea of what he is talking about. For starters, see the Glossary at the back of this book. As you become more involved, get a copy of Langenkamp's *Handbook of Oil Industry Terms and Phrases* or his *Illustrated Petroleum Reference Dictionary* (PennWell Publishing, Tulsa).

Once you have succeeded in finding an operator whose past performance record indicates that he seems to be honest and appears to know what he is doing, you may find that he doesn't particularly want your money. Many successful operators regularly work with a group of investors who have expressed their desire to purchase a small percentage in every drilling project being undertaken by that operator. It may seem odd, but today large amounts of investment capital are available from all kinds of sources, largely because of the quite considerable tax advantages associated with them.

Virtually all exploration activities conducted by independent companies, meaning anyone other than the majors, are financed by private capital. Individuals become limited partners in a specific project which calls for sinking a well or wells on one or several pieces of real estate whose mineral rights have been leased by the operator. The operator, the general partner, usually retains the largest percentage of interest but must also pay the largest percentage of the drilling and completion expenses.

The size of these partnerships in terms of individuals involved and amount of total investment being raised can vary greatly. At the bottom of the ladder are individuals or small companies which may raise as little as $100,000 from relatively few investors for drilling a single exploratory well at a location which appears promising because of the proximity of other producing wells, plus some geological research which the operator paid for prior to acquiring the lease for the mineral rights. At the other extreme are huge drilling funds which may raise as much as $20 million or more for a single drilling program, usually involving several dozen wells to be drilled, both in proven and unproven areas. These companies are registered with the SEC, and much of the investment will be raised through a limited number of selected brokerage houses. While partnerships in the small companies may occasionally be available for as little as $1,000, the large drilling funds usually require a minimum investment of at least $5,000 with additional units available at $1,000 each.

The principal difference from the investor's point of view is that an investment of a given amount in one of the major funds is limited to the amount initially agreed upon, and the investor (or limited partner) is not expected to pay additional funds to cover expenses. This is usually not the case with the smaller operations. Here, the limited partner, whose initial investment was, say, $1,000, will receive monthly statements of the expenses incurred. He is expected to pay his share of these expenses, based on the percent of his interest in the total operation. Thus, what began as a $1,000 investment may end up costing $3,000–$4,000 before there is any return from production, assuming the drilling effort does not result in a dry hole.

But then there are the participatory differences. A $1,000 initial investment in a $100,000 operation buys the investor technically a one-percent interest. In actuality, there is a rule of thumb in the oil business which states that "one-third buys one-quarter." What this means is that the potential profit from an operation actually amounts to a lesser percentage. If your investment represents one-third of the total investment, you'll be paying one-third of the exploration expenses but you'll be receiving only one-quarter of the net revenue. In addition, you'll be responsible for contributing an equal one-quarter to the subsequent production expenses, assuming the well is a producer.

By contrast, a $5,000 (five-unit) minimum investment in a $20 million drilling program adds up to only one-quarter of one-tenth of one percent (0.025%), which, applying the one-third buys one-quarter rule, actually amounts to 0.0209 percent of whatever profit may be derived from the proposed drilling program. On the other hand, the potential for at least limited success is somewhat greater in view of the number of wells being drilled in the context of that single program.

Let's look at the results of two such programs which were conducted in recent years. One program involved 21 drilling prospects on lands to which the mineral rights had previously been acquired.

Date	Description	Debit	Credit
Jan 3	Original investment (1%)	$1,600.00	
Mar 26	D&C equipment	917.31	
Apr 28	Equipment, operation	360.57	
May 25	D&C expense	43.05	
Jun 26	D&C expense	51.41	
Jul 24	Oil run		$258.18
Aug 23	Oil run		176.46
Sep 6	D&C expense	20.36	
Sep 23	Oil run		334.81
Oct 23	Oil run		279.12
Nov 8	D&C expense	21.25	
Nov 23	Oil run		248.67
Dec 23	Oil run		237.11
		3,013.95	1,534.35
First year's unrecouped expense			$1,479.60

(D&C: Drilling and completion)

On these prospective drilling sites, 28 drilling operations took place, resulting in 18 oil wells, 1 gas well, and 9 dry holes. The other program involved 15 sites on which 21 drilling operations were undertaken, resulting in 18 oil wells, 1 gas well, and 2 dry holes. In each case, the investors received somewhere between one-quarter and one-third of their initial investment back within one year from the startup of the operation.

Now, observe the results of two typical operations, one successful and one less successful. The above statement represents a relatively successful operation. Despite the fact that the investor is still out $1,479.60, the well obviously appears to be a continual producer, and the operating expenses—which were initially quite substantial—will be small from now on. Thus, assuming that revenues from oil as well as expenses will continue at the rate established during the last months of that year, the second year and probably succeeding years will bring revenues of approximately $3,000 per year against expenses of about $300 per year, or an annual profit of $2,700. This well produces oil at a rate of approximately 28 barrels per day. It's not sensational, but it's commercially viable.

The next statement refers to a similar operation, except that the oil produced did not justify operating. Here, the initial investment was the same and the operating expenses were practically identical.

Date	Description	Debit	Credit
Jan 8	Original investment (1%)	$1,600.00	
Feb 27	D&C equipment	899.42	
Mar 27	Equipment, operation	372.14	
Apr 25	D&C expense	54.11	
May 26	D&C expense	57.54	
Jun 23	Oil run		$211.12
Jul 21	Oil run		32.12
Aug 5	D&C expense	21.38	
Aug 23	Oil run		15.97
Sep 23	Oil run		32.21
Oct 8	D&C expense	23.09	
Oct 23	Oil run		16.02
Nov 23	Oil run		16.09
Dec 5	D&C expense	26.51	
Dec 23	Oil run		16.17
		$3,051.19	$339.70
First year's unrecouped expense			$2,711.49

The big difference is the amount of revenue obtained from the oil being produced. Even though the well looked pretty promising at first, production diminished to where it was less than the expense of keeping the well in operation. As a result, the partners plugged the well, took their losses, and abandoned the project. Based on the available figures, it would appear that the well was producing oil at the rate of less than two barrels per day.

However, always remember that the initial investment as well as all drilling and completion costs are tax deductible. If you're in a 25-percent tax bracket, you're using 75-cent dollars. The higher your tax bracket, the less you're paying out in money that would otherwise have to go to the government.

Both of these examples were based on actual experiences. Now, assume that your $1,600 investment for a one-percent interest in a similar operation had resulted in a well producing 200 barrels per day—still small when compared to some wells which produce more than 2,000 barrels per day. Two hundred barrels per day would result in a revenue to the partnership of something near $180,000 a month at today's average prices of crude. This would result in a payoff to the one-percent partner (applying the one-third buys one-quarter principle) of $1,503 per month. The average operating expense alloted him would remain at about $300 per year, meaning that for as long as the well continues to produce he could count on a net pretax profit of $17,736 per year ad infinitum. It's arithmetic like this which draws investors to the oil and gas business.

Pyramid it –
drill 10 mo ea year –

8

One-third buys one-quarter

When you first get involved in researching the investment opportunites in the oil business, you'll frequently hear the phrase "one-third buys one-quarter," meaning that if your investment represents one-third of the total investment, you'll be paying one-third of the exploration expenses but you'll be receiving only a quarter of the net revenue and you'll be responsible for contributing an equal one-quarter to the subsequent production expenses (assuming the well is a producer).

Your initial reaction will probably be that you're being cheated somewhere along the line. After all, if you're throwing in one-third of the total, you ought to be entitled to an equal one-third of the profit. Logical as this seems, that's not the way it is.

Take a simple but fairly typical example. Operator Smith has spent $5,000 in acquiring a lease to the mineral rights on a given amount of acreage, and he figures that it will take another $145,000 to drill the first well on that property. He now goes to his investors and tells them that the lease calls for 20 percent in royalties to the holders of the mineral rights, which means that the net revenue from the well will be 80 percent of the total production. He further explains that he is retaining a 25-percent interest in that net revenue, and that for the remaining 75 percent of the net revenue he is seeking an investment of $150,000. This means that in return for putting the deal together he will have a free ride "to the casing point"—all drilling expenses to the predetermined drilling depth.

Suppose there are three groups of investors, each group putting up $50,000. (Each group may consist of any number of individuals, some of whom may actually invest as little as $1,500, which would represent only one percent of the total invested.) This would indicate that each group has invested a third, but that each third bought only a quarter of the potential net revenue because the operator is retaining the additional quarter.

Once the well has been drilled to the casing point, all of that changes. (If it's a dry hole, that's the end of it, of course.) From here on, each group pays only one-quarter of the subsequent costs associated with production, and the operator pays one-quarter just like the rest of them. Conversely, each group of investors is entitled to one-quarter of the *net* revenue from the well, the same as the operator. (In this example, with the holders of the mineral rights getting a 20-percent royalty, each such quarter of the net revenue represents one fifth of the gross production of the well.) If additional wells are drilled on the same acreage, the operator and the investor groups equally share all expenses associated with drilling and all net revenues of the production from these additional wells. Your initial reaction may be that the operator is getting a lot for nothing. But remember, he initially invested his own money for the lease and is the one experienced person who understands this business—and expertise is always worth money.

Be sure to find out where those 20-percent royalty payments go. If they go to the holders of the mineral rights, fine. But if only 10 percent goes to the holders while the other 10 percent goes to the operator or to members of his family, then he is actually reserving 10 percent of the gross plus 25 percent of the net (or a total of 30 percent of the gross) for himself. Unless this is spelled out right in the beginning, something underhanded is probably going on and investors might be justified in questioning the integrity of the operator.

A word about royalties. In years past, a one-eighth royalty (12.5 percent) was considered more or less standard, and many of the preprinted royalty leases still include that figure. But things have changed. Today a one-eighth royalty contract is a rarity. Most mineral-rights holders try to bargain for a greater royalty, and 80, 75, and even 60-percent net-revenue leases are common, meaning leases in which the royalties amount to 20, 25, and even 40 percent of the gross. If the well turns out to be a good producer, even a 60-percent net-revenue lease can prove profitable. But if it's just marginal, then the cost of operating the well may be too great to leave the operator and his investors with a profit after paying that 40 percent off the top.

The increase in the price of oil and the great acceleration in drilling activity have resulted in more unconventional deals. A lot of horse trading is going on, much of it resulting in some pretty complicated contracts. In some cases, there may be an agreement to keep royalty payments low until "payout," meaning until the initial investment in the well has been recouped, with an increased royalty schedule from that point on. Others may call for high royalty payments in the beginning and a downward sliding scale later in case production drops below a certain predetermined amount. The variations tend to be endless, depending largely on the bargaining ability of the people involved. As a general rule, a deal in which the lease calls for a net revenue of less than 75 percent should probably be approached with caution. The lower the net revenue, the longer it will take to recoup the investment and the greater production must be in order to be profitable in the long run. As always, there are exceptions to this rule, but thinking of 75 percent as the absolute minimum is probably a good idea.

The next time someone tells you that your one-third investment buys one-quarter, he isn't trying to skim off some unearned gains for himself; it's simply the way the mathematics work in this business. Think of it along the same lines as you would if you hired a lawyer on a contingency basis: you're paying a percentage of potential profits for the privilege of using someone's expert knowledge.

no - on a contingency a lawyer gets nothing if he fails

9

How much oil must a well produce to be profitable?

The arithmetic involved in determining the eventual profitability of a well is rather complicated. To shed some light on the figures involved, let's take a fairly typical example. Assume we are financially involved in a well which, upon completion, is producing. Prior to putting together his group of investors, the operator had leased 40 acres for his drilling unit, paying a premium of $10 per acre or a total of $400 for the lease, which also stipulates that the lessors receive a one-fifth (20%) royalty. Further assume that the oil being produced is eventually sold for $30 per barrel.

With the signed drilling lease in hand, the operator then gets the appropriate permits and other paperwork involved with a drilling operation. He figures that drilling to the depth which, according to geologist's reports, should be right for the discovery of oil will cost $120,000, including the $400 for the premium on the lease and a small cushion to allow for unforeseen eventualities. He himself will retain a 20-percent interest in the well.

The final investment group consists of one person investing $30,000, representing 25 percent of the total invested and a 20 percent interest in the net revenue from the well. Two persons invest $15,000 each for a 10-percent interest in the net revenue, three investors put up $10,000 each, obtaining a 6.667-percent interest, and 10 individuals put up $3,000 each for a 2-percent participation.

Further assume that the monthly cost of pumping and maintaining the well will amount to $5,000 a year, 20 percent paid by the operator and 80 percent by the group of investors, each according to

Investment	Gross bbl/day	Gross revenue (month)	Net revenue (month)	Interest in net revenue	Net to inves-tor (mo.)	Expense per month	Profit/(Loss) 12 mo.	24 mo.	36 mo.
$30,000	10	$ 9,000	$ 7,200	20%	$83.33	$ 1,440	($ 13,720)	$ 2,560	$ 18,840
$15,000	10	$ 9,000	$ 7,200	10%	$41.67	$ 720	($ 6,860)	$ 1,280	$ 9,420
$10,000	10	$ 9,000	$ 7,200	6.667%	$27.78	$ 480	($ 4,570)	$ 859	$ 6,289
$ 3,000	10	$ 9,000	$ 7,200	2%	$ 8.33	$ 144	($ 1,372)	$ 256	$ 1,884
$30,000	30	$27,000	$21,600	20%	$83.33	$ 4,320	$ 20,840	$81,680	$122,520
$15,000	30	$27,000	$21,600	10%	$41.67	$ 2,160	$ 10,420	$35,840	$ 61,260
$10,000	30	$27,000	$21,600	6.667%	$27.78	$ 1,441	$ 6,955	$23,911	$ 40,866
$ 3,000	30	$27,000	$21,600	2%	$ 8.33	$ 432	$ 2,084	$ 7,168	$ 12,252
$30,000	70	$63,000	$50,400	20%	$83.33	$10,080	$ 89,960	$209,920	$329,880
$15,000	70	$63,000	$50,400	10%	$41.67	$ 5,040	$ 44,980	$104,960	$164,940
$10,000	70	$63,000	$50,400	6.667%	$27.78	$ 3,362	$ 30,007	$ 70,014	$110,020
$ 3,000	70	$63,000	$50,400	2%	$ 8.33	$ 1,008	$ 8,996	$ 20,992	$ 32,988
$30,000	100	$90,000	$72,000	20%	$83.33	$14,400	$141,800	$313,600	$485,400
$15,000	100	$90,000	$72,000	10%	$41.67	$ 7,200	$ 70,900	$156,800	$227,700
$10,000	100	$90,000	$72,000	6.667%	$27.78	$ 4,802	$ 47,295	$104,591	$161,886
$ 3,000	100	$90,000	$72,000	2%	$ 8.33	$ 1,440	$ 14,180	$ 31,360	$ 48,540

his percentage of participation. Thus, the monthly expense is $83.33 for the $30,000 investor, $41.67 for the $15,000 investors, $27.78 for the $10,000 investors, and $8.33 for the $3,000 investors.

According to the chart, if the well would produce ten barrels a day, it would take part of the second year for the investors to get their original investment back and realize a small profit. After that, of course, the profit would continue at a regular rate for as long as the well would continue to produce. If the well produced 30 barrels a day, the investors would make a healthy profit in the first year, and any production in excess of that figure would soon turn each of them into wealthy individuals.

Based on the chart, a well would need to produce approximately 11.5 barrels a day to result in 100-percent repayment of the original investments during the initial 12-month period. On the other hand, a well producing 1,000 barrels a day would produce a gross income of $900,000 a month or $10,800,000 a year. Of this, the lessors would receive $2,160,000; of the remaining $8,640,000, the 20-percent investor would receive $1,727,000 net after covering his portion of the operating cost. The 10-pecent investor would receive $863,500, the 6.667-percent investor would clear $575,955, and the 2-percent investor would get $172,700. This would mean that each investor would get approximately 58 times his investment back in the first year.

Therefore, while a dry hole obviously implies the total loss of all risk capital invested, any reasonable amount of production will, at today's prices, result in an eventual profit. If the quantity of oil being produced is small, however, this profit may be years in coming. This is one additional reason why investors should only use risk capital which they can do without for a fair number of years.

And, of course, not all producing wells continue to produce indefinitely. As an example there is a case on record where the investors were informed at six in the afternoon of one summer day that they had struck oil. They broke open bottles of champagne and celebrated until two in the morning when there was a call from the well: "Sorry, fellows, the well just ran dry." The well had produced a total of 37 barrels of oil; that was all. Even at $30 a barrel, $1,110, that isn't much of a return on a $120,000 investment.

10

Tax incentives, depletion allowance, and the windfall profits tax

Today's tax laws offer a number of advantages and incentives relative to investment in oil and gas drilling activities. As is true of virtually all tax regulations relating to outside sources of income, things tend to get a bit complicated. It might be advisable to consult an accountant knowledgeable in oil and gas exploration tax matters to determine the degree to which tax advantages may be available to the investor, based on the amount of investment.

The initial expenses incurred by the partnership, meaning the general partner and the limited partners, consist of two types of costs: intangible drilling and development costs (IDC) and tangible equipment costs. The latter, reusable equipment purchased by the partnership, is treated much like capital investments are in other industries. It is usually of no interest in limited partnership situations, as independent operators will often employ a contractor who owns this equipment and uses it for each of his drilling assignments. By contrast, intangible drilling and development costs are associated with only one particular operation and have no residual value. They include all monies for labor, repairs, supplies, hauling, fuel, surveying and clearing the ground, constructing roads, cleaning pumps, laying pipeline, and anything else which may be required for eventual oil or gas production.

It is common practice for drilling funds and individual operators to consummate a deal with a drilling contractor in the year in which the fund is set up, even if actual drilling may not be expected to start until the beginning of the following year. In this case, the funds or partnership will prepay the entire amount of the contract at the time of signing; an IRS ruling states that partial prepayment does not qualify as an IDC expense deduction in that year, while full prepayment does. Since the IDC expense, representing from 65–80 percent of the total average cost of a well, is fully deductible, an investor is likely to find oil or gas exploration an attractive risk.

Another important advantage is the result of the depletion allowance. Mineral reserves are finite—depletable—and exhausting these reserves through production is inevitable. With this in mind, the taxpayer is allowed a deduction from the gross income for this depletion. Anyone who has acquired a proportionate ownership in mineral reserves through financial investment and who must look for the return of his investment to the income which can be derived from the extraction of such minerals is entitled to take advantage of the depletion allowance. At current rates, it amounts to 22 percent, meaning that 22 percent of the gross income derived from the production of oil or gas may be considered nontaxable. According to present tax laws, the 22-percent rate will be reduced to 20 percent in 1981, 18 percent in 1982, 16 percent in 1983, and 15 percent in 1984 and after.

And then there is that famous windfall profits tax. It is one of those political hybrid monstrosities to which a democratic society is subject and which ends up producing results that are diametrically opposed to the original intent.

President Jimmy Carter was faced with the problem of initiating legislation which would induce the major oil companies as well as the independents to increase exploration activity, hoping this increased activity would eventually result in a reduction of the country's dependence on foreign oil. The obvious answer was deregulation of the price of domestic oil to let it gradually climb to the level of the price of foreign oil. This meant that everyone involved in the oil business would be able to make the kind of profits which justify spending the huge amounts of risk capital required for subsidizing major wildcatting operations, especially offshore and in other inaccessible areas.

But then came all that media exposure of the rapidly rising net profits of the major oil companies, profits which politicians described as "obscene." Granted, profit figures by Mobil and Exxon, running into 100-percent increases and millions of dollars, struck the average reader and TV viewer (i.e., voter) as abnormally high. Unfortunately, emphasis was placed on the companies' initial profits, not on the dividends for thousands of stockholders and the billions of dollars spent exploring offshore in the Atlantic or in other unexplored areas. Carter was fully aware that reports of these tremendous profits on the heels of doubling gasoline prices would be blamed on his deregulation of domestic oil; therefore, he politically had to do something to reduce that negative impression.

Most Americans do not understand what the oil business is all about. Therefore, they think that those oil-company "profit machines" create problems at the service station. So when the government decided to punish the oil companies for making "all that money" by creating the windfall profits tax, everyone was elated. The Administration was finally hitting those gluttonous oil companies where it hurt with an excise tax while producing a quarter of a trillion dollars in revenue over the next decade. In other words, it was killing two birds with one stone.

Except that one of the birds isn't getting hit by the stone. It is actually ricocheting onto the average consumer, who always ends up paying the bill. In its final form, the bill Congress approved (remember, this was just prior to a major national election) hurt primarily the small independent operators who don't own refining plants and thousands of gas stations and can't pass the cost on to the consumer. Of course, investors also felt the impact as their royalties shrunk. The majors, on the other hand, could charge the consumer for that money they have to turn over to the government. If results run true to the past, their profits will continue to grow.

But the fact everyone overlooks when these figures are cited is that these profits are our only hope for eventually climbing out from under the yoke of foreign oil-producing countries. Wouldn't it, in the long run, be better to pay all that money to the oil companies which then spend most of it in the U.S. by reinvesting it in exploration and production activities designed to make us eventually energy self-sufficient than to spend it lining the bottomless coffers of OPEC? Wouldn't it be better than giving those countries the opportunity to buy up huge amounts of U.S. real estate or to acquire the controlling interest in major U.S. corporations with money which was originally yours and mine?

Take, for example, the scope of drilling operations which major oil companies conduct within one area of the world: the Gulf of Mexico. On any day or night, seven days a week, there are about 26,000 workers living and working offshore. Approximately 250 drilling rigs are drilling new wells at various locations in the Gulf, some as far as 200 miles out at sea. Over 2,200 structures, platforms, and caissons including 1,100 production platforms with heliports serve the 5,835 producing wells from which 21 million barrels of oil and 350 million cubic feet of natural gas are fed each month into a network of 11,500 miles of pipeline. In order to find those 5,835 producing wells, over 16,000 wells were drilled, two-thirds of which were dry holes. The mineral rights which are owned by either state or federal governments are expensive. In one case, one company paid $973 per square foot for a 5,000-acre block, totaling $212 million. In order to transport men, women, and material in the process of serving this vast complex, only one of several helicopter operators uses 474 helicopters which transport approximately 147,000 passengers per month, flying an average of 25,000 hours. Each of these helicopters costs over $1 million to purchase, and their operation and maintenance costs run into hundreds of dollars per hour. While none of this is of any direct consequence to us as potential or actual investors in the oil business, it does provide an insight into the reasons why a barrel of oil costs so much.

These are the kinds of figures people forget when they think of the big oil companies. They overlook the tremendous expenditures the companies are making, trying to find new oil and relieve our dependence on foreign suppliers. The windfall profits tax hurts no one but ourselves.

However, the windfall profits tax is law today, and for the time being we're stuck with it. It wouldn't be so bad if all that money were earmarked for developing alternative energy sources. But based on the subsequent actions of the Congress with funding research and development, the money is simply going to end up in the General Fund where it will eventually be frittered away by bureaucratic inefficiencies, while having an adverse effect on the rate of inflation. Hopefully, the next Administration will rectify this mistake and modify or revoke the tax.

11

Case histories

When you ask an oilman what your chances are of getting a return on your investment, assuming you want to take a chance on a drilling project, his answer will probably be one in nine. These odds have become a rule of thumb in the oil business, but they are no more reliable than the odds of throwing a seven at the dice table (7 to 1). As any inveterate crapshooter knows, there is no assurance that seven rolls of the dice will necessarily produce one seven. Similarly, an investment in each of nine drilling projects will not necessarily produce one profitable well.

In order to provide a clearer picture of what might (and then, might not) happen, we will use the next few pages to give the details relative to several investments in drilling projects. Some represent investments in major drilling funds while others refer to small independent operators. All are based on fact, though care has been taken to avoid identifying the individuals or funds involved.

I

Jane Brown got a divorce from a husband who had turned out to be the kind of man she had no intention of spending the rest of her life with. The divorce settlement left her with $40,000 in cash which she felt she didn't really need to live on, since her income as a real-estate broker took care of the day-to-day expenses, not counting the child-support payments which would take care of her teenage daughter.

Listening night after night to newscasters talking about double-digit inflation, she decided that keeping this money in savings accounts paying less than the current rate of inflation was stupid. On the other hand, the type of real estate she was dealing with on a daily basis usually ran into $80,000 to $200,000 figures, meaning that the best her $40,000 would be able to buy her would be a partial interest and a mortgage with monthly payments in some type of relatively low-yield income property.

In discussing her problem with friends, she ran into one who had been lucky in oil after investing less than the amount of money she had available, so she decided that she might as well take a chance. She was smart enough to realize from the very beginning that she might end up losing every nickel, but she also figured that the chances of making a killing were worth the risk. Before taking the first step she talked to her accountant who told her that, based on her current income-tax bracket of roughly 30 percent of her adjusted gross income, each $1,000 invested in oil would, in fact, cost her only $700. Based on that she figured that she would actually be able to invest a total of $57,000 before using up all of the $40,000 risk capital at hand.

Living far away from Texas or any other place where oil is a subject that is discussed at cocktail parties, she looked through the Yellow Pages under "Stockbrokers" and, after calling several, found one who claimed to be knowledgeable in the subject of investing in oil. They met at his office where he tried to explain the difference between investing through a drilling fund and with individual entrepreneurs, suggesting that a drilling fund might be the better suggestion. He admitted that he, himself, was not representing any of the drilling funds, but explained that an associate in a nearby city might be able to help.

To make a long story short, she eventually learned about a drilling fund which was in the process of putting together a drilling program and which was in the market for investors at a minimum investment of $5,000. She was also told that this drilling fund, as well as most others, made it a requirement that investors either have a net worth of $200,000 or more or be in the 50-percent tax bracket. She realized, of course, that she could not qualify on either of these counts, forgetting for the moment that her 80%-paid-for house might just have brought her close to qualifying for the $200,000 requirement.

But quite aside from that, Jane was enough of a businesswoman to know that any claims she might make about her net worth or income-tax bracket would be accepted without a great deal of scrutiny. She thus handed a $5,000 cashier's check over to the broker and in good time received the appropriate papers which stated that she owned five units of interest in the drilling program which was scheduled to close in another month and planned to start drilling activities within the following twelve months on a number of drilling units.

The brochure which she had received prior to making her investment had been rather specific in pointing out the risks involved and had spelled out whose money was going to pay what percentage of which expenses and what the investor's percentage of eventual revenues would be. While she found it difficult to relate all of these percentage figures to her own minute contribution to the total fund, at least she felt that she wasn't jumping in blindly. What she read was that, with reference to the costs, the general partner (the drilling fund itself) would pay only one percent of offering costs, sales commissions, and management fees while the remaining 99 percent would come out of the capital supplied by the limited partners, namely the individual investors. The cost of acquiring the leases, drilling, and completing the wells, 85 percent of which were supposed to be in areas of known reserves while 15 percent were described as wildcats, was to be paid in a ratio of 20 to 80, meaning that the drilling fund would pay 20 percent and the investors would pay for the remaining 80 percent. The same proportion was to apply to something described as "all other costs" which didn't mean much to her. And then there were two categories described as "ordinary operating costs" and "general and administrative expenses" of which the fund would pay 35 percent while the limited partners would be charged with the remaining 65 percent.

She was somewhat more interested in what it said about who was going to get how much of the revenues which might result from the drilling program. Here the figures appeared less confusing. Revenues from oil, gas, or any other minerals would be divided 35/65, meaning that the fund took 35 percent and the investors would get 65 percent. Other potential revenue items such as something described as "revenues from the sale of leases, plant, property or equipment" and "all other revenues" seemed to her to be of little if any interest.

She realized, of course, that her money and that of her fellow investors would be used to pay 80 percent of the lion's share of the expenses, while she would be receiving only 65 percent of any possible profits, but she assumed, correctly as it was, that this was more or less standard procedure. Based on some of the past history of the drilling fund, which was set forth in considerable detail in the brochure, she decided to go ahead, believing that the chances of losing her entire $5,000 investment were actually quite small. She was enough of a realist to not expect to make a sensational killing. After all, she still had $35,000 left to play with in the future (plus whatever tax savings her investment produced), and she figured that this might give her an opportunity to learn what the oil business was all about.

In terms of dollars and cents, here is what happened. The total investment by the limited partners was $1,000,000. The value of each $1,000 unit of investment was 0.1 percent. And the value of Jane's $5,000 investment was 0.5 percent.

	Net revenues distributed to limited partners	**Jane's portion**	**Profit (loss)**
First year	$253,976	$1,270	($3,730)
Second year	$381,764	$1,859	($1,871)
Third year	$315,998	$1,580	($ 291)
Fourth year	$338,773	$1,694	$1,403
Fifth year	$419,893	$2,099	$3,502
Sixth year	$425,718	$2,129	$5,631

What this shows is that it took Jane a little over three years to get her original investment back and it took close to six years to make a 100-percent profit. And for this she had, to some extent, to thank the increase in the prices paid for crude oil. Without those increases it might have taken several more years to make a comparable profit.

But in the meantime Jane had learned quite a bit about the oil business, and she decided to use whatever returns came her way as the result of the original $5,000 investment as additional risk capital by investing it with several small independent operators. By asking questions of friends and acquaintances and writing letters to some of the independent oil associations, she eventually made contact with an operator who was in the process of putting together a drilling program.

By taking all of her first year's receipts and a portion of the second year's, she invested $1,600 for a one-percent interest, aware that in this case she would also be responsible for part of the operating costs in the event that the drilling program should prove to be successful. Several months later, having been assessed another $403.12 in additional drilling and completion costs, the hole turned out to be dry. By now she had received a total of $3,129 in returns from her initial investment and she had spent $2,003.12 of that on a dry hole. But she felt that she was still $1,125.88 ahead of the game and those monthly checks, averaging a little better than $100 a month, kept coming in. So she figured that she might as well try again.

During the six-year period covered by the figures shown above, she invested in a total of five drilling projects, three of which turned out to be dry holes, one produced barely enough oil to cover its operating expenses, but one, the fourth in the group, proved to be a good one. It produced over 200 barrels a day, resulting in a monthly income in excess of $1,000.

By now she has given up her real-estate activities, spending most of her time reading oil-industry magazines and reports, always looking for additional promising investment opportunities. She had caught the oil fever. But being a basically sensible type, she continues to limit her investments to the amounts available from the revenues from previous investments, never touching her initial capital or whatever amounts she knows she'll need to live on for the next year or so.

II

Homer Ferguson and his wife Betsy own a 20-acre farm in Nebraska. The land has been in Betsy's family for several generations and has provided them with a fairly good living, good years making up for the occasional bad ones. The year when this story took place was beginning to show all the signs of again being one of the bad ones.

One day, a couple of fellows showed up on the Ferguson spread and introduced themselves as representatives for an independent oil company. They inquired if the Fergusons owned mineral rights to their north 20 acres.

"That's right, we do. Why?"

"Our company has acquired a lease of the mineral rights to the west and north of your farm and we're planning to sink an exploratory well about 1,000 feet or so from the northwest corner of your property. We'd like to lease the mineral rights to your 20 acres for a year. We're authorized to give you a check right now for $12 per acre, that's $240, and a contract which will entitle you to your share of the royalty profits in case we do discover oil or natural gas."

"What exactly do you mean by our share?"

"Well, the leases which we have already cover 40 acres. If we add your land, that'll make that 60 acres. The standard royalty for the entire acreage is 12.5 percent or one-eighth of the gross receipts from any production. That means that you'd be entitled to 4.1667 percent of the total production or one-third of one-eighth."

"If we go along, does that mean you're going to put one of those ugly towers up on our land?" It was the first time that Betsy had entered the conversation.

"Well, it would give us the right to do so within the year covered by the lease."

"I don't like it. It just doesn't make sense to take a silly amount like $240 and then let people drive their trucks all over our fields and put up one of those awful contraptions in our backyard."

"Any harm we might do to your land, Mrs. Ferguson, we'd of course restore or pay to have restored, and once we find oil, the derrick would then be removed."

"I still don't like it."

The two visitors looked at each other and suggested that the Fergusons discuss it between themselves.

Later that evening Homer and Betsy were sitting in their favorite chairs, he smoking his pipe, she busy mending something.

"You know, dear," Homer muttered, "it could be worth a lot of money."

"Two hundred and forty dollars is a lot of money?"

"I don't mean that. I mean if they do find oil."

"Nonsense. There hasn't been any oil around here in a hundred years. What makes you think those fellows know what they're talking about?"

"Yes, there was. Remember, back there in the '50s they found some oil about thirty or forty miles north of here."

"Sure I remember. Lasted for maybe six months or so and then they said it wasn't worth bothering with so they shut the thing down. This drilling notion is crazy."

"Well, I guess technically it's your land, so you've got to make the decision."

"And I say no."

"Maybe you're right. Only, what if . . ."

"What if, what if. If it'd rain tomorrow, we'd have a good year. Only, it isn't. Homer, we've done okay all these years and we're gonna continue to do okay. I just don't want nobody to mess up my land is all."

"Okay, if you say so."

As it happened, the first well on the adjacant land was a dry hole, and Betsy was pleased to be able to say, "I told you so." But undaunted by the initial failure, the company drilled a second well—a producer. Not exactly a spectacular one, but one which gave all the indications that it would continue to produce at a moderate rate for many years to come. This time it was Homer who said, "I told you so." But by that time there had been rain and the year looked as if it weren't going to be a total loss after all, so neither of them worried much about the loss of any income from oil.

They had just about decided to forget about the whole incident and to chalk it up to experience when two other fellows showed up. They explained that, based on what had been learned from the one successful well, there was a good probability that a well placed on the Ferguson land, some considerable distance from the house, would also hit oil. This time they made the lease offer a bit more attractive and even added an extra overriding royalty offer. Even though Betsy still wasn't happy with the idea, she finally gave in and agreed to sign the papers.

Today, the Fergusons still farm their land as they always have, only they have all kinds of new farm machinery and equipment, all fully paid for. There are no longer those annual bank loans to worry about, and if the rains don't come when they should, it's no longer as serious a problem. Even though they are psychologically incapable of thinking of themselves as potential millionaires, that's exactly what they are. And while Homer doesn't mind driving out and watching that pumper do its thing, hour after hour, Betsy never goes near it.

III

Harry Smith liked to gamble. At every conceivable opportunity he would show up in Las Vegas where, more often than not, he'd lose more money than he won, though he always managed to kid himself into believing that he'd at least broken even. It was there that he got into a conversation at a bar with a fellow he had watched earlier wagering large sums at one of the high-stakes tables.

"Looks like you're doing all right," he commented while the other man took out a hundred-dollar bill to pay for his drink.

They chatted for awhile, and eventually Harry learned that his new friend was in the oil business.

"You mean you go out there and drill holes in the ground?"

"Uh-uh. I just put up some money, that's all, and when they find oil, I get paid every month for as long as it keeps pumping."

"What happens if they don't find oil?"

"Then I'll try again."

"Seems to me that's not much different than throwing your money on the crap table."

"That's where you're wrong. Here, if you get three or four times your money back you're damn lucky. Me, I started with 20 grand ten years ago and right now I'm working on my third million."

Harry didn't really believe him, but he couldn't help being fascinated. So they decided to have dinner together and by the time they parted company Harry knew what he was going to do: he was going to clean out his savings account and turn himself into an oil millionaire.

At first he wasn't any more lucky in oil than he had been in Las Vegas. Several initial investments turned out to be dry holes. His money was running short and he decided that if the next one didn't bring in any money, he'd better quit. But the next one did produce oil and for a while it looked as if he'd finally hit a winner. He was already making big plans about what he would do with all the money he'd be making when, after having produced a little over 300 barrels, the well simply quit. That was all, there wasn't any more.

Now, if this well had been a dry hole from the beginning, Harry might actually have quit. But having tasted even this small bit of success, he simply knew that the next one would be the big one, so he talked his banker into lending him $10,000 and, using it plus whatever meager funds he still had left, he picked a drilling program which he felt in his bones would be a success and bought himself an eight-percent interest.

Another dry hole.

By now he knew that he was in trouble. His savings account was defunct and he owed the bank $10,000 which he didn't know how he was going to pay. But like any true gambler he knew that he couldn't quit now. How did that old saying go? Quit when you're ahead, but when you're behind, no way!

It took awhile, but there came a time when Harry seriously considered talking to an attorney specializing in bankruptcies; for months he had been afraid to answer the phone because he was running out of excuses when all those bill collectors started to get ugly. He was flat broke. He'd managed to borrow $2,000 from someone who had once been a friend by virtually getting down on his knees. It had been dropped into one more hole which, if past history would repeat itself, would also turn out to be dry.

Well, Harry's luck had just been dormant. The hole turned out to be a well, and the well was a good one. Today, just two years later, Harry is starting to work on his second million. All his bills are now paid, his loans have been returned plus interest, and the phone number of that bankruptcy attorney has found its way into the wastebasket. Knowing Harry, he'll probably dump much of his sudden wealth down a lot more dry holes, but as long as his one good well keeps pumping (and indications are that it will continue to do so for more years than he expects to be alive), it would require more foolishness than even Harry is capable of to again put him on the doorstep of the poorhouse.

12

Summary

Oil and natural gas investments are a gamble. Like all gambles, they may pay off and then again they may not. When they don't pay off, the wager is lost irretrievably down the drain; but when they do pay off, chances are they will continue to do so for years. There are lucky investors who become overnight millionaires, and then there are others who foolishly overextended themselves and lost their shirts.

THE DECISION TO INVEST

In order to invest in oil or natural gas, one need not be a special kind of person or be unusually wealthy to start with, but a degree of discipline on the part of the potential investor is needed. The inveterate gambler, the kind who would mortgage his car or home for just one more last stake at the gaming tables, should stay away from the oil business. Investing in oil tends to be habit-forming, and there have been cases of investors who, after a series of dry holes, found themselves facing bankruptcy. Some were lucky enough to be bailed out by one last desperate investment which resulted in a producing well which made them rich. Others went under.

That's where the discipline comes in. A firm decision should be made at the outset, placing a limit on the amount of money which can be safely gambled away without affecting the lifestyle of the investor and his family. And that decision should be adhered to religiously. The person who remains steadfast stands the best chance of eventually coming out on top.

MONEY

The money to be invested should be funds which are not needed to pay for the necessities of life—funds which are lying fallow in a savings account or under a mattress, losing value with every increase in inflation. It does not have to be a huge amount, but there should be enough to permit participation in more than one or two drilling operations. A one-percent interest in such an operation may require only $1,000 or $1,500, but the chances of one such investment being successful are slim. In order to reduce the risk to an acceptable minimum, the potential investor should have sufficient funds available to participate in about 10 wells. With a one-percent interest in each of 10 drilling operations, assuming the operator has a good track record, the chances of making at least one hit are fairly good.

With this in mind, the amount the investor should probably have is at least $15 000, preferably a little more. Carefully spread around, it may still be a total loss, but chances are that it will not. Remember, always use discretion. Find an operator with a fair percentage of successes and then stick with him.

When that one well out of 10 does come in, the earnings from that well can be used for additional investments. At that point, you're playing with house money and there is no further need to touch your own capital, but still keep the investments small and numerous. Always remember that one percent in a producing well is a lot better than 10 percent in a dry hole.

TAX ADVANTAGES

Drilling, operating expenses, and related costs associated with investments in the oil business are tax deductible. Thus, depending on the tax bracket of the investor, he will actually only pay a certain percentage of the total amount of the investment. A person in a 30-percent tax bracket will be using 70-cent dollars, while a person in a 50-percent tax bracket will actually pay only half of the investment out of his own pocket.

And there is the depletion allowance. A certain portion of the income derived from oil or natural gas is exempt from taxes. As a result, success in the oil business produces double advantages in terms of tax benefits, advantages which are not available to a comparable extent with most other investment opportunities. When the time comes, consult a tax accountant knowledgeable in oil. Things tend to get a bit complicated and the cost of expert advice is always money well spent.

INFLATION

A huge variety of investment types is touted these days as effective hedges against inflation. Most of these involve purchasing items which increase in value faster than the rate of inflation. In order to take advantage of them, the investor must eventually find a buyer for his purchase. Not so with oil and natural gas. Instead of items to be hoarded and eventually sold at a profit, oil and natural gas pay off handsomely from the very first day and in many instances continue to do so. There simply is no other type of investment which represents a hedge against inflation that can compare with the opportunities associated with oil and gas.

INVESTMENT OPPORTUNITIES

There are two basic types of investment opportunities available to the average investor: drilling funds and independent operators.

Drilling funds are large operations which generate million-dollar investments and use them to drill a predetermined number of wells, usually in several different locations. These funds have hundreds of individual investors for each announced drilling program, and they operate under the supervision of the Security and Exchange Commission. The minimum investment in drilling funds is usually $5,000 or more, and such investments can be arranged through reputable brokers. While the eventual payoff in terms of percentages of the oil or gas being produced is somewhat less than from investing with independent operators, the investor knows that the sum involved is fixed and he will not be asked to make any additional payments in the future.

Independent operators are small companies which put together drilling programs whenever the rights to drill on a selected piece of acreage are obtained. Each drilling program initially involves only one well; all costs associated with the drilling of that one well are borne by the investors while the independent operator has a free ride up to the production point. If the hole is dry, that is the end of it. If it's a producer, the independent operator and his investors share equally in the expenses associated with completing the well and the subsequent expenses associated with continuing production. If additional wells are drilled on or adjacent to the original acreage, no additional investment is called for, except that the operator and his investors share equally in the expense associated with those additional wells.

As a general rule (there are exceptions), the investors as a group, having paid 100 percent of the cost of drilling the initial well, are entitled to 75 percent of the net return derived from production while the operator takes 25 percent, and the costs associated with completion and production are shared at the same percentage rate. Net production usually represents between 87.5 percent and 75 percent of the total production, the rest going as royalties to the holders of the mineral rights.

THE END OF THE RAINBOW

What is the potential profit associated with investing in oil? There is no way of telling, because no two successful drilling projects produce the identical results. But here are a few figures which might prove helpful.

In each instance, we assume that the investor has bought a one-percent interest and that his share of the continuing production expense is $400 a year. We further assume that the well is drilled on acreage which calls for a 20-percent royalty, meaning that the net production is 80 percent of the total.

What this shows is that while a marginal well will return some profits, it takes a fair amount of production to get a truly meaning-

Gross prod. bbl/day	Net prod. bbl/day	Net prod. bbl/year	$ for net prod. year	1% interest*	Less $400 cost of operation
10	8	2920	87,600	627	227
20	16	5840	175,200	1,314	914
30	24	8760	262,800	1,971	1,571
50	40	14600	483,000	3,623	3,223
70	56	20440	613,200	4,599	4,199
100	80	29200	876,000	6,570	6,170
300	240	87600	2,628,000	19,710	19,310

*In view of the fact that the operator retains a 25-percent interest in the net production of the well, the one percent interest actually only represents 0.75 percent (see chapter 8).

ful return on the investment. This is one of the reasons why successful investors keep using their profits for additional investments until the cumulative total of production reaches a certain plateau. Because of the tax advantages these figures are actually better than they look on paper.

APPENDIX A

A typical description of a proposed drilling project

What follows is more or less typical of the kind of information which an independent operator might supply to prospective investors. It is taken from an actual case, though the names and locations have been changed to maintain confidentiality. Any interested investor, especially one dealing with a given operator for the first time, should request this type of information and should study it carefully before committing himself.

ABEL PROSPECT
Abel County, Oklahoma

Location

The Abel Prospect is located in western Abel County, Oklahoma, on the southeast flank of the Baker-Charlie Basin. The town of Abel is southeast and adjacant to the acreage block. U.S. Highway 99 is about one-half mile from the proposed drill site and a gas pipeline parallels the highway. An oil pipeline is located about four miles north of the block.

Stratigraphy

The targets at the Abel Prospect consist of five separate zones within the D and J sands of Cretaceous age. Each must be considered a primary target based on a combination of structure, stratigraphy, and/or shows. A brief discussion of the stratigraphy of each prospective zone follows.

D-1

The key control point, spotting in the NE Section 7, penetrated a total of 18 feet of D-1 zone, of which 13 feet showed microlog porosity. No apparent shows were observed in a core of the interval.

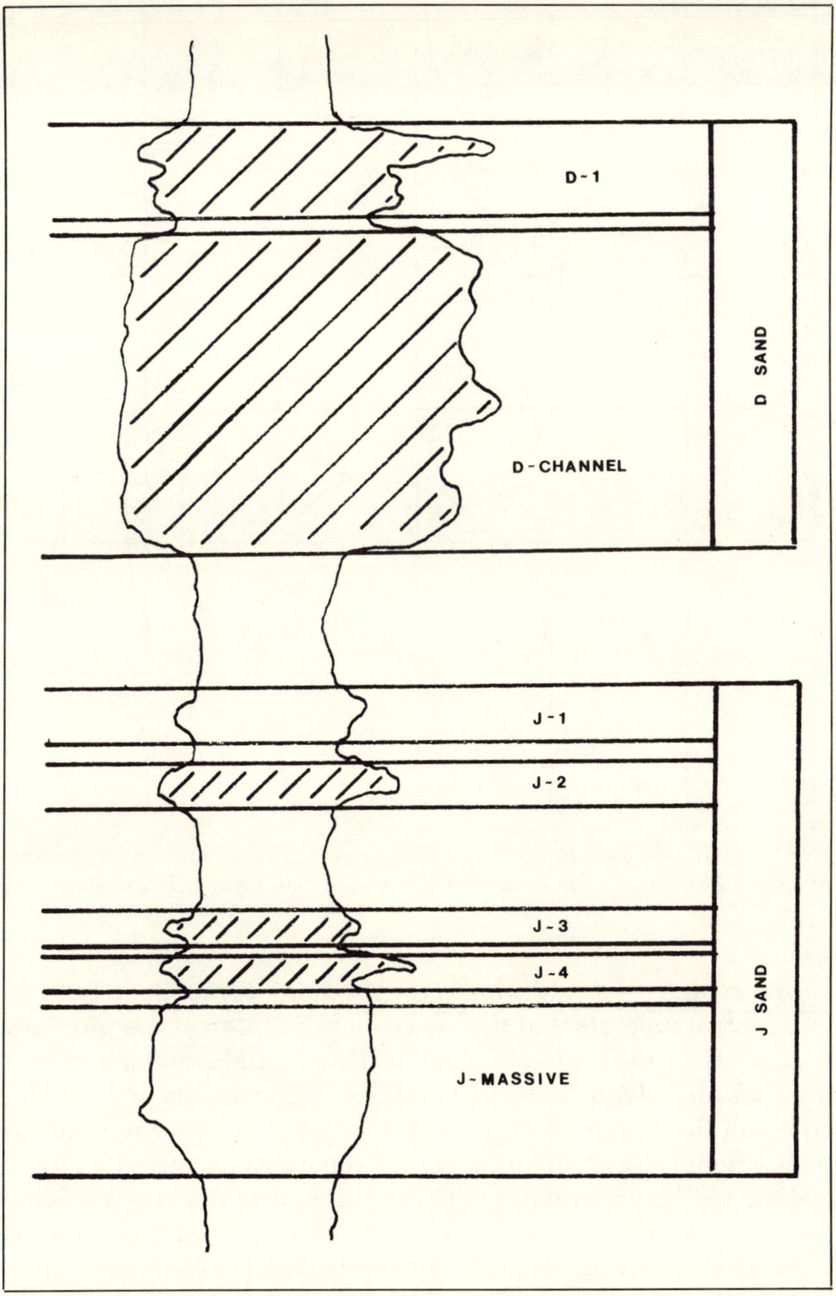

The drilling targets in the Abel Prospect.

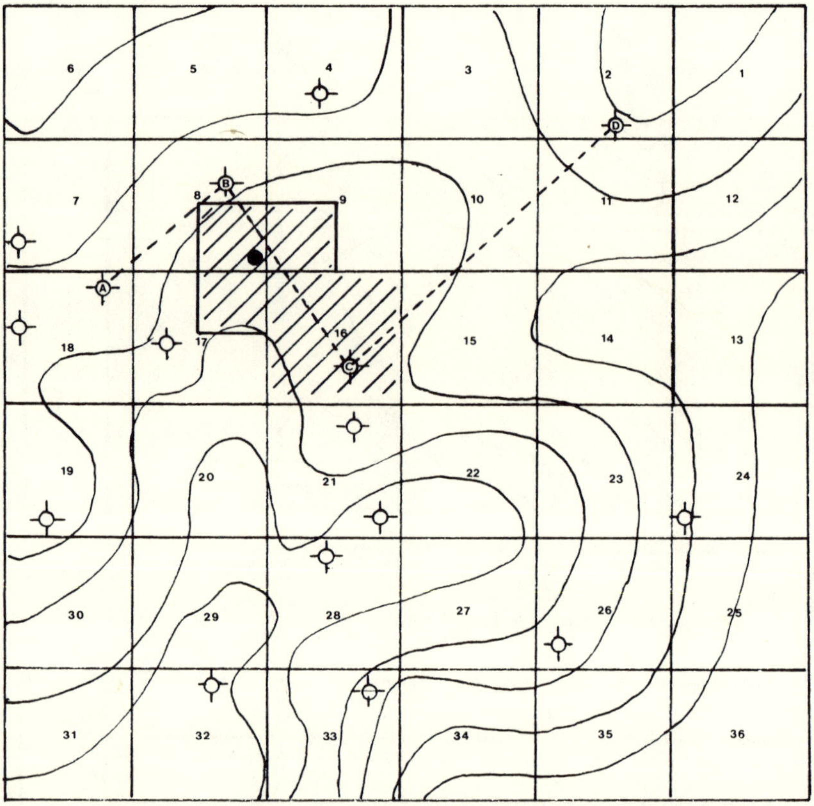

Map showing the location of the Abel Prospect relative to previous drilling attempts. The ● is the location of the proposed drilling site. The -ф- marks dry holes.

Porosities and permeabilities ranged from fair to excellent. Subsurface control suggests that this sand is a bar deposit and is probably younger than the regional upper D. Differential compaction over the thick underlying D channel in the key well possibly provided for an ocean floor high and a locus for a higher energy environment than is found elsewhere in the area. Even if this theory is incorrect, and the D-1 here correlates with the regional, updip control shows the D-1 to be tight and a trap would be provided. Lack of shows is negative evidence for this unit but surely does not condemn it. In a high-quality reservoir, such as this, the oil-water transition is thin and a few feet of structural gain could result in production.

D-CHANNEL

The D-channel sand play in the Abel area is probably the highest risk of the five prospective zones, but at the same time it offers the most potential in reserves. The key well penetrated 66 feet of excellent-quality sand. The upper 16 feet were cored and the core was examined. The top foot had slight shows (weak spotty fluorescence, no cut). The channel is mappable in the area and runs northwest-southeast. Five tests penetrated the channel in the township, and four of these carried shows. The main question regarding the potential of the channel is whether the updip marine "country rock" enclosing the channel will provide a barrier. The critical updip test, spotting in Section 16, is tight in the upper two-thirds of the D, but the lower portion has porosity.

J-2

The J-2 sand is considered to be the lowest risk target at the Abel Prospect. In the key well this zone was cored. The scout ticket describes it as "7½ sand, fair to good, P & P, fine to medium, friable, yellow fluorescence." The writer was able to obtain core samples from only the top foot of the sand, which is described as follows: Sand, light grey, lower medium grained, fair to well sorted, good to excellent porosity and permeability, even yellow fluorescence, fair milky cut, very light stain. The microlog-caliper shows about 8½ feet of porosity which was not drillstem tested. The strength of the core shows indicates that a few feet of structural gain would result in a discovery. This sand is developed only in the key well, and the "trend" of the sand cannot be determined. The key updip test, in Section 16, penetrated a silt zone in the equivalent interval which strongly suggests proximity of sand development, as other nearby tests penetrated only a shale section.

J-3 & J-4

These sands will be discussed together as they are very similar. Both sands were cored in the key downdip test in Section 8. The J-3 was described on the scout ticket as "5′ sand with light to medium oil stain, spotted stain in streaks, light spotted yellow fluorescence." The J-4 was "2½ sand, reworked, dead oil stain, brown to yellow fluorescence; 4 sand, good P &P, fractured, shale partings." Unfortunately this core was not available for examination by the writer. The key updip test in Section 16 did not go deep enough to correlate definitely with the test in Section 8. It appears, however, that the silt zone some 20 feet above total depth may be equivalent to both the J-3 and J-4, in which case a trap is provided. The sand right at total depth could be either the J-massive or the J-4. The high resistivity of this sand suggests it may have a "log show." No porosity log was run. The core shows in both the J-3 and J-4 again suggest structural advantage over the test in Section 8 would result in production.

Structure

The structure map shows a broad arch trending northeast-southwest diagonally across the township. This feature is well substantiated in the immediate area as well as semiregionally with established subsurface control. The main axis appears to trend across the Able Prospect acreage block. I have interpreted a closure centered along the boundary between Section 9 and 16. The presence of a closure would, of course, be ideal, but it is not necessary for entrapment in any of the five zones discussed. The downdip test in Section 8 penetrated five sands that are absent in the key updip test, and four of these sands carried shows. There are 27 feet of structural relief between the two tests. Assuming some reversal, if not closure, between the two, on the order of 50 feet of structural advantage over the test in Section 8 can be anticipated.

Economics

The nature of the prospect, with several prime potential pay zones, makes economic analysis difficult. For our purposes, we will calculate only the potential reserves in the J-2. Assuming 8 feet of net pay and 250 barrels per acre foot recoveries, a 40-acre location should produce some 80,000 barrels of oil worth about $1,670,000 to the working-interest owners, assuming $25.00 per barrel of oil. The J-2 and J-3 together would provide an additional 10 feet of pay. The D potential is more difficult to estimate, but it could be very substantial.

Assuming 640 acres productive, the J-2 alone could produce some 1,280,000 barrels worth about $38,323,000 to the working-interest owners.

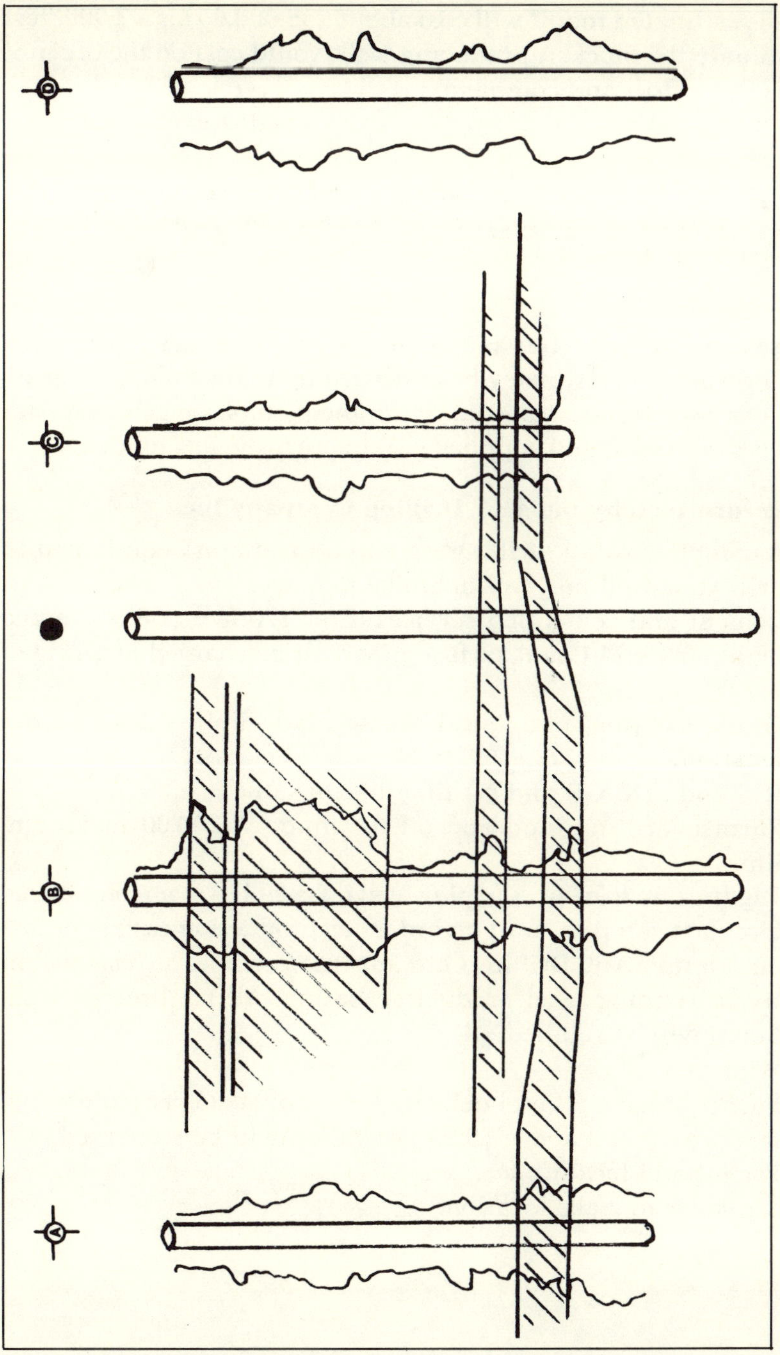

Chart showing the expected subsurface structure in the area in which the proposed well is to be drilled.

It is estimated that it will cost about $55,000.00 for a 3,900′ test to evaluate the block. A producing well would cost on the order of $150,000 to drill and complete.

Signed: John S. Doe

Also included in the information provided to potential investors is a bid from a reputable drilling company which would read more or less as follows:

Dear Mr. Doe:
Please consider this letter as a bid to drill the well, described as the Abel Prospect, on a turnkey basis according to the following specifications and terms. Material, equipment, tools, machinery, appliances, services, and supplies will be furnished as follows:

To be furnished by the ABC Drilling Company Inc.

(a) A complete rotary drilling rig and all necessary equipment to drill your well in a workmanlike manner.
(b) Cement and cementing services (first 270 feet of 8⅝″ surface pipe); any additional surface pipe will be charged at a rate of $12.00 per foot.
(c) Grade location, pits, build access road, limit of $500.00 per location.
(d) IES and FDC GR and rig time to run same.
(e) Furnish drilling mud and oil for mud; $1,200.00 maximum limit.
(f) Rig time up to 6 hours to plug well if dry hole, to run long string, circulate samples, wait on orders or production casing, or lost circulation. ABC Drilling Company Inc. assumes no responsibility in running used production casing. All rig time over six hours will be rebilled.
(g) Water.
(h) Fuel is based on diesel delivered price of $0.93 per gallon. Any increase in fuel above $0.93 per gallon will be recharged.
(i) Permit and location fee.
(j) Surveyor to stake location.

ABC Drilling Company Inc. agrees to assume all responsibilities and liabilities as an employer and otherwise as to social security, unemployment, withholding, and other taxes assessed by law or other regulatory bodies upon the properties or operations of the ABC Drilling Company Inc.

To be furnished by the operator

(1) Surface and crop damage to landowner.
(2) Right-of-way for roads and location.
(3) Geologist and core lab expenses.
(4) All catwork and towing of trucks above first $500.
(5) Backfill pits.
(6) All logging charges except those designated by the Contractor.
(7) Daywork rates will be charged after first 6 hours of lost circulation, plus lost-circulation material, water, and truck time to haul water.
(8) Pay for all third-party services in completion of the above well which include, but are not limited to, cement, cementing services, casing crews, casing and other materials needed for completion work, or pump truck to plug a dry hole; all costs and rig time upon failure of used production casing.

This well will be drilled to 3,950 feet, or 100 feet below the top of the J Sand Formation, whichever comes first.

Turnkey price for the drilling of this well will be $41,500.00 for services as set out above.

Turnkey price for each successful DST will be $3,100. All attempted DSTs that are not successful will cost $2,200. The cost of a Straddle Test will be $3,500.

Mileage of $0.75 per mile will be recharged for tester. Bottom hole sampler and extra charts not included.

Daywork rates will be $1,960.00 with or without drillpipe.

This bid expires 15 days from the date of this letter.

Yours very truly,
ABC DRILLING COMPANY, INC.
Signed: John Smith, President

A third piece of information included in the presentation will probably be a schedule of the leases which have been obtained by the operator, giving the dates on which the leases were signed, and the term of each lease for each portion of the drilling unit. It might read something like this:

LEASE SCHEDULE

Harry and Mary Jones	SE/4 8	7/24/80	3 years
Bruce and Anna Adams	SW/4 9	7/26/80	3 years
State of Oklahoma	All of 16	7/15/80	10 years
XYZ National Bank, Trustee for B.C. Baker Estate	NE/4 17	8/11/80	3 years

All this information coupled with previously obtained knowledge of past successful activities by the operator should give the investor whatever background he or she needs in order to decide whether or not to participate in the venture.

APPENDIX B

Progress reports

Once drilling has started, all operators will provide each investor with periodic progress reports, usually on a weekly basis. What follows is one such report, typical of the type which the investor can expect to receive, no matter the size of his investment in the project.

To all investors—Baker investments #1, Charlie County, Texas

The Baker No. 1 was spudded in on September 17, 1979, and reached a total depth of 6,117′ on October 5, 1979.

The primary objective Canyon reef limestone was encountered at 5,944′, or 53′ high to the nearest well located 1,100′ to the north. A drillstem test in the first reef porosity (5,947′–5,957′) had gas to the surface in five minutes (gauged at a rate of 280 MCF per day on ⅝″ choke), and recovered 630′ free oil and 120′ heavy oil and gas cut mud. Initial and final shut in pressures were 2,610# and 2,574# respectively. A second drillstem test from 6,018′ to 6,038′ recovered 610′ of gas in the drill pipe and 62′ of slightly oil cut mud. A third drillstem test from 6,074′ to 6,100′ recovered 386′ of gas in the drill pipe and 610′ of salt water.

At total depth Schlumberger induction-electric and density logs were run and a dipmeter survey taken. The logs indicate 9′ of productive section from 5,949′ to 5,958′. We are setting production casing today and expect to complete in the next few days. We believe we have a good well, and should be considering offset drilling in the next few months in view of the early expiring leases.

Additional potentially prospective acreage which we may want to acquire appears to be available in the area. Thus, I think it is best that we all exercise prudence by not divulging this well information to others, at least at this time.

Sincerely yours,
(signed) John Jones

A point well taken here is that it would behoove all concerned to not rush out and shout the apparent success of the well from the nearest rooftops. In a case like this, where adjacent acreage appears to be available for mineral leases, it would be more intelligent to keep quiet until the well has proven out and, beyond that, until those additional leases have been signed.

APPENDIX C

Typical offerings by drilling funds

The first reproduced here represents a relatively small drilling fund which is not and does not intend to be registered with the S.E.C. All names and locations are fictitious.

CONFIDENTIAL PRIVATE PLACEMENT
MEMORANDUM

35 Undivided Nonproducing Fractional Working Interests in Tracts Located in Beta County, Kansas. Minimum Purchase—One (1) Unit at $8,600.00 per Unit. Maximum of Thirty-five (35) Participants.

These are speculative securities in that they involve a high degree of risk.

This memorandum is not a prospectus nor does it constitute an offer to sell a fractional undivided working interest. The information contained herein is for the confidential use of the recipient and may not be reproduced or copied in any manner whatsoever.

Any distribution of this memorandum to any person other than the person whose name appears hereunder, or the divulgence of its contents in whole or in part, without the prior written consent of the program sponsor is prohibited.

	Offering price to participants	**Organizational expenses**	**Net proceeds to be used for drilling and completion**
Per unit:	$ 8,600.00	$ 1,032.00	$ 7,568.00
Total:	$301,000.00	$36,120.00	$264,880.00

The undivided, nonproducing fractional working interests referred to herein have not been registered under the Securities Act of 1933 or the securities laws of any state.

Submitted to:	XYZ OIL COMPANY, INC.
(name)	(address)

XYZ OIL COMPANY, INC. is offering thirty-five (35) Units consisting of fractional nonproducing working interests in the lease comprising the Program Acreage. The subscription price of a Unit is $8,600.00 per Unit. Each Unit constitutes 2.8571% of the working interest or 2.2857% net revenue interest in production from the leases until pay-out, at which time XYZ Oil Company, Inc. will be entitled to a 25% reversionary working interest which equals a 20.000% reversionary revenue interest in the production from the leases.

This offering involves certain speculative considerations. Because of these considerations, no person should purchase the units which are offered hereby unless he is financially able to sustain a total loss of his investment. Moreover, because of substantial restrictions of the transfer of these units, each investor should be prepared to hold this investment for an indefinite period of time.

This memorandum is intended solely for the inspection of the person to whom it is addressed. Its reproduction or circulation to other parties has not been authorized. The receipt of this memorandum constitutes the agreement of the offeree to return it to the company in the enclosed envelope in the event that the offer is not accepted. No dealer, salesman or other person has been authorized to give any information or to make any representations other than those contained in this memorandum. Specifically, but not by limitation, no person has been authorized to make any projections with regard to this project. If any such information is given, it must not be relied upon as being authorized by the company. Except where otherwise indicated herein, this memorandum speaks as of its date.

Offering summary

The following summary is included only as a quick reference guide. All prospective purchasers should carefully examine the entire memorandum prior to acquiring an interest in this project.

ISSUER:	XYZ OIL COMPANY, INC. (address)	
UNITS OFFERED:	35 units of undivided working interest. Each unit represents 2.8571% or the working interest or 2.1857% of the revenue interest.	
PURCHASE PRICE	Per Unit	For 35 Units
Drilling & testing, completing & equipping	$8,600.00	$301,000.00

Use of proceeds

Funds available from the sale of the units offered will be applied to drilling, testing, completing and equipping the wells in Echo 1. Funds for such purposes will be available from the subscriptions of the investors hereto. Any amount not required for the stated purposes will be retained by XYZ OIL COMPANY, INC. and the company will have no obligation to account to investors for any amount so retained. If the costs of drilling and testing and completing and equipping the wells exceeds the amount assessed the investors as set forth in this offering, XYZ OIL will assume the costs and there will be no additional assessment to investors.

Risk factors

1. No guarantee of production: The proposed drilling program has been designed to drill five oil wells on a proven field, known as the Beta Oil and Gas Field. Nevertheless, the business of oil and gas exploration and production is known for its risks, and there can be no assurance that production can be obtained.
2. Insurance: The company will have liability insurance with respect to drilling and operating the properties involved. However, if uninsured risks are encountered or the limits of such insurance were exceeded, the investors could be subject to liability for such risks.
3. No transferability: The units of undivided working interest which are offered hereby will be issued under a restrictive endorsement, which will preclude their resale or transfer

without registration under the Securities Act of 1933, unless an exemption therefrom is available and an opinion to such effect is obtained from counsel for the company. There can be no assurance that such exemption will be available. Moreover, it may be expected that there will be no market for these units. Accordingly, only persons who intend to maintain their ownership for an indefinite period of time should consider the purchase of these units.

4. Dependence on contract personnel: The company will be significantly dependent upon the technical services of its personnel and the death, disability or separation from service of any such personnel could adversely affect the success of the proposed program. Further, the company independently contracts for such services as drilling, testing, completing, and equipping the wells and consequently must rely upon the knowledge, skill and expertise of others.
5. Tax matters: Although it is believed that the investors hereto may be entitled to report several items as deductions from their gross taxable income, the possibility exists that all or part of these potential tax benefits may be modified or discontinued through actions of Congress or the interpretations rendered by federal or state regulatory bodies. Therefore, XYZ OIL COMPANY, INC. can give no assurance as to the availability of any tax savings from investment in this profit.

Description of drilling program

The Echo 1 Prospect is located approximately (geographical coordinates and detailed descriptions of the prospect location). The prospect is part of a certain field known as the Beta Oil and Gas Field.

The Beta Oil and Gas Field was drilled extensively during the early 1900s. It was originally a number of separate fields that were eventually joined together to become one large continuous field. The field has produced many millions of barrels of oil since its discovery. During the past few years there has been renewed interest in the field primarily due to the increased price and demand for production and the known existence of commercially productive oil in the field.

The primary objective of the program is sand known to be lying at a depth of approximately 850 to 950 feet where it exhibits substantial thickness.

It is the general thesis that the field has not been drained by any previous drilling and that commercial production can be obtained from the prospect.

XYZ OIL COMPANY, INC. will drill and, if warranted, complete five wells on the Echo 1 lease to a depth sufficient to test the sand, plus a sixth well to be used as a disposal well. Drilling sites will be chosen by the company. Completion will be attempted on the wells if the information obtained from the sands appears adequately positive. It is anticipated that the wells will be completed, however there can be no assurance that any Echo 1 well will be commercially productive. On the well, if completion is not attempted, the sum of $6,200.00 will be refunded to the investors hereto, pro rata.

At the time and if production is commenced, the company will deliver to each investor an assignment of oil and gas lease, representing such investor's undivided interest. These assignments will be in recordable form. XYZ OIL COMPANY, INC. intends to make available to the investors in Echo 1 the opportunity to have their proceeds from any production disbursed through the trust department of a bank, who may then deduct the monthly operating expenses, including the bank's monthly service fee, and remit the net proceeds to the working-interest holders on a monthly basis. All disbursements under this procedure will be made according to the generally accepted accounting practices.

The company, at its sole discretion, shall determine that the well is no longer commercial, and shall thereupon proceed to abandon and plug such well. Plugging expenses shall be shared by the owners of the working interest in accordance with their respective interests, and any proceeds accruing from the sale of salvage equipment and casing shall be distributed in the same manner.

Terms of the offering

(Here the document repeats at considerable length what has been stated above with reference to nonregistration with the S.E.C. and to the fact units are nontransferable and are not being sold through salesmen or dealers.)

In order to satisfy the conditions of these exemptions and to insure that any tax benefits available may be fully utilized, these units will be sold to no more than thirty-five (35) individuals who certify to XYZ OIL COMPANY, INC. that:

1. The units are being acquired solely for investment with no view towards redistribution, and
2. That his net worth exclusive of his home and automobiles exceeds $200,000.00, or
3. That his net worth, exclusive of his home and automobiles exceeds $50,000.00, and that a portion of his current income will be subject to taxation at a rate of at least fifty percent (50%).

No less than one (1) unit of working interest will be sold to any investor and fractional units will not be offered or sold. XYZ OIL COMPANY, INC. reserves the right to accept or reject the subscription of any investor hereto.

This drilling project will not be commenced until thirty-five (35) units of working interest have been sold. XYZ OIL COMPANY, INC. reserves the right to purchase units for its own account.

Description of securities offered

The investors hereto are acquiring undivided working interests in the oil and gas leases covering the 80 acres subject to the XYZ OIL COMPANY, INC. lease. Of the full 100% revenue interests, the owners of the working interests as a group shall be entitled to 80%. The balance of the revenue interest is held by the land owners in the form of a 12.5% basic royalty and overriding royalties in the amounts of 3.125%, 3.125%, and 1.25%. The owners of the royalty and overriding royalty interests are entitled to receive their proportionate share of production. Thus, the holders of the working interest will bear 100% of the costs of production and be entitled to 80% of the production revenues until payment.

XYZ Oil Company's revisionary interest

The company is offering the full 100% of the 100% working interest on the 80% net revenue lease. After the investors as a group have recovered their investment, the company will retain 25% of the working interest, and investors as a group shall own 75% of the working interest.

Distribution of Proceeds—Working Interest

	Before Payout	After Payout
Per unit	2.8571%	2.1428%
Investors as a group	100%	75%
XYZ Oil Company, Inc.	0%	25%

Since each investor's $8,600 purchase represents 2.8571% of working interest, at a price of $33.50 per barrel, at least 10,000 barrels must be sold before the investor will begin to realize a return on his investment exclusive of costs of production.

The investors are acquiring an interest in the Echo 1 Program and are not acquiring any interest in the company itself. Accordingly, any profit or loss of his investment will be limited to the success or failure of the Echo 1 Program.

(Here follows another long paragraph dealing with the fact that the securities obtained by the investors are not transferable. This paragraph is followed by a brief history of the company and biographical sketches of the officers and staff of the company.)

Assignment

In the event commercial production is obtained, XYZ OIL COMPANY, INC. will forward a properly executed assignment in recordable form to each working-interest holder. XYZ OIL COMPANY also intends to offer bank trust disbursement of said proceeds if desired by the investor.

Compensation

XYZ OIL COMPANY, INC. will retain a 25% revisionary interest in the Echo 1 project. After each investor has recovered his $8,600.00 per-unit investment, XYZ OIL COMPANY, INC. will be entitled to 25% of the working interest production revenues, and will bear 25% of the operating costs.

If the actual costs of drilling and completing the wells in the Echo 1 Program meet the estimated costs ($301,000) XYZ OIL COMPANY will retain out of the proceeds of this offering a total of $36,120 for organizational expenses. Moreover, if the actual drilling and completion costs are less than estimated, all funds which are not so utilized will be retained by XYZ OIL COMPANY, INC.

Conflicts of interest

XYZ OIL COMPANY, INC. could realize revenues from the proceeds of this offering without regard whether or not the proposed drilling program is successful.

XYZ OIL COMPANY, INC. shall be free to engage in other drilling projects including projects in the area of the Echo 1 Program. The investors hereto shall have no guaranteed right to particpate in such projects.

Reports and records

The company will notify investors when and if all units have been sold, and will render drilling-progress reports thereafter on a weekly basis during drilling operations.

The company will furnish monthly production reports, and prior to (date) of each year will furnish investors with sufficient information to include on their personal tax returns. This yearly report will include a summary of the receipts and disbursements from the Echo 1 account.

The company will maintain records with respect to the Echo 1 Program at its headquarters office. Those records may be inspected by any investor during normal business hours.

Tax matters

At the present time considerable uncertainty exists as to the tax consequences of oil and gas investments such as the Echo 1 Program. For that reason each investor should consult his personal tax counselor. All items of deductible expenses will be for the account of the investors hereto as to their availability or extent of such deductions. XYZ OIL COMPANY, INC. has a synopsis of a tax opinion which is available upon request.

Additional information

This offering contains a fair summary of the matters referred to herein. Persons to whom offers are made will be furnished with such additional information concerning the project, XYZ OIL COMPANY, INC., or other business matters as they or their business, tax and legal advisors may reasonably request. They are urged to make such personal investigations, inspections and inquiries as they deem appropriate.

(With reference to all of the above, also see the operating agreement, appendix D.)

The following is a summary of an offering by a drilling fund which is registered with the Securities and Exchange Commission. Each unit offered represents an investment of $1,000, but a minimum purchase of five units ($5,000) is required. The total prospectus covers some 88 printed pages, amounting to something like 75,000 words. It is too long and detailed to be included here, but the following summary gives a relatively clear picture of what is involved. Investors who are interested in making investments through such a fund are urged to read the prospectus covering a given drilling program from cover to cover.

AAA FUNDS–1980 PROGRAM

(Minimum Subscription $5,000)

Summary of program

Terms of the Offering: An aggregate of $20,000,000 in performation limited partnership interests, consisting of 20,000 units at $1,000 per unit, are being offered by AAA Oil Company (the General Partner) in up to three limited partnerships to be formed for the purpose of engaging in the acquisition and development of oil and gas properties. The partnerships will be formed pursuant to the Partnership Agreement set forth in Exhibit 1 to this prospectus, and, except for possible variations in capitalization, will be structurally identical. Each participant must purchase at least five units for an aggregate purchase price of $5,000 and may purchase greater amounts in multiples of one unit ($1,000). A partnership will not be formed until subscriptions for not less than 1,000 units, aggregating $1,000,000, have been received. Subscriptions are payable in full upon execution of the Subscription Agreement. The subscription period may be terminated by the General Partner at any time after $1,000,000 in subscriptions have been received. The subscription period for the second partnership shall commence after termination of the subscription period for the initial partnership, and the subscription period for the third partnership shall commence after the termination of the subscription period for the second partnership. In the event a partnership is not formed, all amounts subscribed will be promptly returned in full with interest earned, if any. A participant will become a Limited Partner in only the partnership to which his units relate. Until formation of a partnership, all participant's funds paid in respect of subscriptions will be held in a special account pursuant to an agreement with the (name of bank and location). Such amounts will be invested in interest-bearing instruments by the bank upon the request of the General Partner, and will not be subject to debts or obligations of AAA Oil Company. Unless extended for a period not to exceed 60 days, the first partnership offering will terminate no later than 90 days from the date of this prospectus. Units are offered on a "best efforts" basis by selected broker-dealers who are members of the National Association of Security Dealers, Inc. Each such soliciting dealer shall be entitled to receive a cash commission of 8% on sales of units by such dealer.

Subject to certain conditions and limitations, the General Partner is obligated to purchase units presented to the General Partner by the Limited Partners.

No additional assessments may be levied against any Limited Partner in connection with the operation of the partnerships.

The General Partner will contribute an amount equal to 20% of the total expenditures of each partnership for costs of acquiring leases and the drilling and completing of partnership wells and 35% of both general and administrative expenses and the ordinary operating costs incurred by the partnerships.

Suitability Standards: This offer is made only to persons acceptable to the General Partner and otherwise eligible to purchase units in the partnerships under state security laws. Those standards of suitability of investment and additional representations and warranties required of Limited Partners by certain states which vary from those imposed by the General Partner are set forth herein under Special Instructions.

Compensation: The General Partner will receive a one-time management fee equal to 4% of the Limited Partners' capital of each partnership. The General Partner will also be reimbursed for the actual offering costs in an amount not to exceed 1% of Limited Partners' capital. The General Partner will also be allocated 35% of the total partnership oil, gas and other mineral revenues, 20% of all partnership costs of acquiring leases and drilling and completing wells, and 35% of the general and administrative expenses and ordinary operating costs incurred by the partnership.

Participation in Costs and Revenues: The Limited Partners will bear 99% of the 8% sales commission payable to soliciting dealers, and the General Partner shall bear 1% of such commissions. The offering costs (up to an amount not to exceed 1% of Limited Partners' capital) and the management fee will be borne 99% by the Limited Partners and 1% by the General Partner. The Limited Partners will bear 65% and the General Partner will bear 35% of ordinary operating costs and the general and administrative expenses allocated to the partnerships. All other partnership costs will be borne 80% by the Limited Partners and 20% by the General Partner. Revenues from oil, gas and mineral sales shall be shared 65% by the Limited Partners and 35% by the General Partner. Revenues from the sale of oil and gas leases, plant, property or equipment shall be shared 80% by the Limited Partners and 20% by the General Partner until recovery of the costs of such property, which have not been deducted for tax purposes. Proceeds of such sales in excess of such costs shall be shared 65% by the Limited Partners and 35% by the General Partner. All other partnership revenues will be shared 80% by the Limited Partners and 20% by the General Partner.

Application of Proceeds: The total net proceeds to a partnership from the partnership capital will be between the maximum of $22,045,000, assuming all units are sold, and the minimum of $1,102,250, after deducting the 4% management fee payable to the General Partner, the maximum of 1% of the Limited Partners' capital for the offering costs, the 8% sales commissions, and adding the General Partner's capital. It is intended that, of such net proceeds, a partnership will expend approximately 85% for acreage and drilling costs associated with wells on proven or semiproven acreage, and approximately 15% for acreage and drilling costs associated with wells on exploratory acreage. The actual application of such net proceeds may vary substantially.

Tax Ruling: A ruling to the effect that each partnership will be treated as a "partnership" and not as an "association taxable as a corporation" for federal income tax purposes has been applied for from the Internal Revenue Service. If the requested ruling is not issued prior to the termination of the subscription period for the initial partnership, the General Partner intends to rely on the opinion of counsel as to the tax status of the partnerships.

APPENDIX D

Operating agreements

Once an operator has put a deal together, every investor is provided with a copy of an operating agreement. These agreements vary considerably in complexity. Those quoted below are relatively typical.

The first agreement quoted below involves 35 investors who jointly put up $160,000 in amounts which bought participations ranging from 21 percent down to ⅓ of one percent.

GULF INVESTMENTS, INC.
OPERATING AGREEMENT

Parties, properties and interests:

This operating agreement between (name of the operator) whose address is 1111 Main Street, Center City, Texas, herein called the operator, and (list of the names of all investors), herein called nonoperator (whether one or more, each party, irrespective of number, sex, or status, being referred to herein by masculine singular pronouns) in reference to the following property in Baker County, Texas:

(Here follows a detailed description of all the leases obtained by the operator for the purpose of this drilling project)

herein called the lease (whether one or more), which lease, together with the equipment thereon, is owned as tenants in common by the parties hereto as follows:

(Here follows a list of the names of all the investors in each instance giving the percentage held by the particular investor. Also listed is the operator along with the percentage he is retaining for himself)

WITNESSETH:

1. APPOINTMENT OF OPERATOR:

   a. Designation of Powers: Subject to the provisions hereof, the above named operator is hereby designated to control and conduct all future development, producing, maintenance, and other operations on the lease, and is granted full power to do whatever is necessary or proper to that end, except that, without nonoperator's approval at the time, operator shall not:

      1) Drill, deepen, rework, plug, or pull the casing from any well;
      2) Incur any single item of expense in excess of twenty-five hundred dollars ($2,500.00) unless such item is incurred in the course of drilling, deepening, reworking, or plugging a well which has been approved;
      3) Carry insurance other than workmen's compensation in accordance with applicable laws: Public liability and property damage insurance;
      4) Employ attorneys;
      5) Compromise any suit or disputed claim;
      6) Abandon the lease;
      7) Dispose of equipment; or
      8) Market production.

   b. Acceptance: Operator accepts the following designation, assumes the burden of such obligations, and agrees, subject to preventing causes beyond his control, to carry out and conduct the same in accordance with the best engineering and accounting practices and applicable governmental regulations, and further, that the lease shall be open to nonoperator at all times, who upon request shall be furnished any desired information, including complete samples and copies of all well logs.

2. TERM:

The term of this agreement shall be concurrent with the life of the lease, or any part of it, and any renewal of it, provided however that any party, at any time, may terminate this contract in its entirety ninety (90) days after written notice to all other parties of such intention.

3. RECORDS, BILLS, AND ACCOUNTS:
   a. Records: Operator shall keep, and there shall be available to nonoperator for inspection at any time, complete records of all operations on the lease, and detailed, itemized accounts showing all costs and expenses incurred, and all income received. Copies of any of such records shall be furnished nonoperator at any time or times upon request.
   b. Advances by Operator: Operator shall promptly pay, within discount days, all costs and expenses (including ad valorem taxes) incurred. Should operator default on any such payment, the same may be discharged by nonoperator, who, in such event, shall be subrogated to the rights of persons so paid, and shall be immediately repaid by operator.
   c. Reimbursements by Nonoperator:
      1) Billing:
         a) Direct costs: On or before the 25th day of each month operator shall mail nonoperator an itemized statement of all costs and expenses, except overhead, incurred and paid on, or for the account of the lease during the preceding calendar month, and of any income which may have been received during such month, (excluding income from production) and shall bill nonoperator for his part of the excess of such costs and expenses over such income, nonoperator's part being the same as his above stated undivided interest in the lease. Such costs shall include the salaries of the operator's geologists, engineers and employees on the lease, with the number of days actually spent by such employees during such month in work on the lease, the cost of number of days in such month, together with the actual expenses incurred by such employees in such work on the lease, the cost of travel in operator's motor vehicles to be computed at (x cents) per mile and (x dollars) per day per man.
         b) Overhead: Except as above provided, the foregoing charges against nonoperator shall not include any part of operator's overhead expense, including all salaries, wages, and expenses of all officers and employees of operator, and all rentals, supplies, maintenance, and

other costs of all offices, camps, and other facilities of operator, who or which serve both the lease and other property in which nonoperator has no interest. In lieu of all such costs the following monthly charges shall be made and nonoperator shall be billed for his said part thereof:

(1) For each drilling well, while drilling: $500

(2) For each producing oil well, not to exceed five such wells while producing: $100

(3) For each producing well in excess of the number set out in the preceding subdivision while producing: $100

(4) For each gas well, while producing: $100

2) Payment: Each such statement shall be presumed to be correct unless objected to in writing within thirty days after its receipt, within which time such statement shall be paid.

d. Interest, Liens, and Attorney's Fees: After default in the payment by any party of any amount due another party hereunder such amount shall bear interest at the rate of (x percent) per annum, and shall be secured by a first lien here now granted the creditor party by the defaulting debtor party against his entire interest in the lease and in the equipment thereon and the production therefrom. If such claim is placed in the hands of an attorney for collection, ten percent of the amount of principal and interest then due thereon may be added and collected as attorney's fees.

4. DIVISION AND SALE OF PRODUCTION:

All production shall be run and sold under division orders executed by all parties, each of whom shall be paid direct for his part of such production by the purchaser.

5. SALE OF INTEREST:

Should any party determine to sell his interest, or part thereof, in the lease, he shall first offer the same for sale at the price and on the terms which he will accept, to the other party hereto, which nonselling party, for five days thereafter, shall have the right to make such purchase. Should such nonselling party refuse, or neglect for said five day period to accept such offer, the selling party shall be free for sixty days thereafter (but no longer) to make such sale to any third person at the same or any higher (but no lower) price, and upon the same or any better (but no poorer) terms. No sale to a third person shall be made until after the nonselling party shall have been afforded the refusal thereof in the manner above set forth.

6. SELF-EMPLOYMENT:

Operator may employ his own services and install his own equipment, but in such event the cost thereof shall not exceed the cost at which like services and equipment are then currently and readily obtainable from third persons, and transportation charges on operator's equipment, irrespective of point of origin, shall be measured from the nearest point at which like materials are available.

7. INVENTORIES:

Once each year operator shall take an inventory of all equipment and other property owned by the parties hereto on the lease. Nonoperator shall be given reasonable notice of, and afforded an opportunity to attend, the taking of each inventory and shall be furnished a copy thereof.

8. COMMUNICATIONS:

All notices and other communications between the parties shall be effective if mailed to the addresses above set out, or to any changed address of which written notice shall have been given.

9. CONSTRUCTION:

The parties hereto are tenants in common only. Neither this agreement nor performance hereunder shall be interpreted as creating any relationship giving rise to joint liability. None such exists or is intended, and one party shall not be liable for the debts or obligations of another. This contract shall be construed as a covenant running with the title to the lease, and shall be binding upon, and inure to the benefit of, the heirs and assigns of the parties. Time is of the essence hereof, and all of the obligations hereunder are performable on the lease.

10.

If any party hereto shall refuse to join in any proposed attempt to drill, deepen, plug back, or work over any well situated on the premises, he will thereby agree that those parties who shall undertake such proposed activity may do so at their sole risk, cost and liability, and may use any existing well bore for workover, plug back or deepening and the casing and other equipment in and upon said well without any change in ownership; and the parties who shall undertake such proposed operations shall receive all leasehold revenues from production thereby obtained until they have received therefrom all (100%) costs of any newly acquired surface equipment beyond the wellhead connections in addition to all expenses of current lease operations and double (200%) the expense and cost of drilling, reworking, deepening or plugging back, testing and completing said well, and double (200%) the cost of newly acquired equipment in the well (to and including the wellhead connection). Pursuant thereto each party agrees that failure to participate in such proposed activity will constitute the assignment of his interest (and also any overriding royalties, production payments or other charges against same if placed upon his interests after the date of this agreement) in such well and the production thereof until the above stated proportion of expenses shall have been recovered. As a condition, however, to effectiveness of this paragraph, it is stipulated that such proposed activity must have been commenced within sixty (60) days of the date such activity was initially proposed, and it is further stipulated that if any party hereto shall not respond to such a proposal within twenty (20) days after delivery of such written proposal to his usual mailing address it shall be conclusively presumed that said party does refuse to join therein.

11. TAXES:

Operator shall render the entire lease on behalf of all owners. The parties hereto specifically elect that operations hereunder be excluded from the application of partnership provisions of the Internal Revenue Code, and each co-owner reserves unto itself the right to make all elections under the said code.

12. EFFECTIVE DATE:

This agreement shall become effective on (date).

(Space for signatures)

Don't blame me for the convoluted language and often capricious punctuation. This document was obviously authored by a bunch of lawyers who were being paid by either the word or the hour. But since much of it is an often used standard form, it might be worth the trouble to study it. In its standard printed version much of it is in very small print and can easily be overlooked.

The next agreement, though also written by an attorney, is a lot easier to read. It deals with a somewhat larger operation in which an equal number (maximum 35) of investors are expected to provide a total of $301,000, with the minimum investment being $8,600. It includes a number of provisions which are absent in the above, and should be throughly understood by interested investors before the offer is accepted. One of the provisions of this agreement empowers the operator to spend less than the total amount of the investment on drilling operations, but permits him to retain any amount not so spent. Technically this might entitle him to spend only a fraction of the investment and to retain the balance as a profit (with no risk) to himself. Whenever such a provision is included in this type of agreement, the investor should be sure to investigate the past-performance record of the operator, as some have been known to make most of their profits from the investments rather than from speculative drilling activity. If we're going to make investments in this business we'll want to invest in oil exploration and the potential profit to be derived from it, rather than in the overhead and profit of the operating company.

Subscription agreement and power of attorney

The undersigned hereby acknowledges that he has received a copy of the offering memorandum of XYZ OIL COMPANY, INC. (the Company) concerning its offer to sell units of undivided working interest in the Echo 1 Project in the principal amount of $301,000.00.

Subject only to the acceptance hereof by the Company, the undersigned subscribes to the principal amount of the units set forth below, which amount the undersigned has paid in full to the Company, receipt of which is acknowledged by the Company's acceptance.

Units purchased: ______________________________

Amount of subscription: ______________________________

In connection with this subscription, the undersigned hereby makes the following acknowledgements and representations:

1. I understand that the offering is being made pursuant to the exemption from registration with the Securities and Exchange Commission afforded by Section 4(2) of the Securities Act of 1933, as amended relating to the offer and sale of securities in a transaction not involving any public offering. Consequently, the Memorandum has not been subject to the review and comment by the staff of the Commission, the Securities Commission of any state, or the National Association of Securities Dealers, Inc.
2. The units which I am purchasing are being acquired for my own account of investment and not for any purpose of resale, distribution, subdivision or fractionalization thereof.
3. I understand that the assignment of working interest, when and if issued to me as a result of a sale made hereunder, will bear the following restrictive endorsement:

    The interest represented by this assignment has not been registered under the Securities Act of 1933. This interest has been acquired for investment and may not be sold or transferred (other than by operation of law) unless, (i) a registration statement covering such interest under the Securities Act of 1933 and any applicable state securities act becomes effective, or (ii) an opinion of counsel for XYZ Oil Company is obtained to the effect that the registration of such interest is not required under such acts.

    Transfer of this interest is further subject to the terms of a certain subscription agreement which is on file with the Secretary of the Company at its home office.
4. I understand that I must bear the economic risks of the investment for an indefinite period, because these units have not been registered under the Securities Act of 1933 and, therefore, are subject to restrictions on transfer such that my interests may not be sold or otherwise transferred (other than by operation of law) unless they are registered under the Securities Act of 1933 or an exemption from such registration is available. The Company has no present intention to file a registration statement under such Act or to comply with Regulation A or any other disclosure exemption under such Act. Securities Act Rule 144 would presently be inapplicable to resale of the units.

5. I have read and understand the contents of the offering memorandum (appendix C) and am aware of the risks associated with the proposed drilling venture. Nevertheless, it is my decision to purchase the units offered hereby, it being my judgment that I am financially capable of sustaining the total loss of my investment; and I submit the attached questionnaire to the Company with the understanding that they will rely on such information.
6. I understand the Company may elect to drill offsets or test deeper horizons in the subject property. In such event, I may participate in the development in accordance with my interest. If I chose not to particpate in the development, I will forfeit my right to production from such development.

Appointment of attorney-in-fact

I do hereby appoint XYZ OIL COMPANY, INC. to act as my exclusive agent and attorney-in-fact, and do grant to said company the sales and exclusive right to act on my behalf in all matters relating to the testing, operation, production, development, abandonment and sales of any or all properties in the Echo 1 Program.

I do further appoint XYZ OIL COMPANY, INC. to act on my behalf to collect all revenues and pay all operating costs and expenses attributable to my interest in the Echo 1 Program and to remit the net revenues to my account on a monthly basis.

The powers above granted are given in consideration for the acceptance by XYZ OIL COMPANY, INC. of my subscription and shall therefore be deemed coupled with an interest and shall be irrevocable.

DATE: ___________ (Space for signatures)

Offeree questionnaire

XYZ OIL COMPANY, INC.
(Address)

Gentlemen:

I have received from you a copy of the Confidential Private Placement Memorandum (the Memorandum) dated (date) covering 35 undivided nonproducing fractional working interests or "Units" in a private five (5) well drilling program designated the

XYZ OIL COMPANY ECHO 1 PROSPECT (the Program) to be organized, conducted and operated by XYZ OIL COMPANY, INC. (the Operator).

I understand that it is contemplated that interests or Units in the Program will not be registered under the Securites Act of 1933, as amended (the Act), or any other state's blue sky laws. I also understand that in order to insure that the offering of these interests shall be exempt from registration under the Act, you are required to have reasonable grounds to believe, and actually believe, prior to making an offer, that all prospective offerees are able to evaluate the risks and merits of an investment in the Program or are able to bear the economic risk of such investment.

I further understand that the information supplied in this questionnaire will be disclosed to no one other than the president of XYZ OIL COMPANY, INC. and its authorized representatives and counsel to the Operator, without my consent, or unless it is necessary for the Operator to use such information to support the exemption from registration under the Act and applicable state securities laws which it claims for the offering.

Please print or type. If the answer to any question is "none" or "Not applicable," please so state.

1. Name: ______________________________
2. Social security number or Tax ID: ______________________________
3. Permanant residence ______________________________
4. Age: ______________________________
5. Occupation: ______________________________
6. Business address: ______________________________
7. Employer or business association: ______________________________
8. Business or professional education and the degrees received:

School — Degree received

____

____

9. Prior employments, positions or occupations during the past five years (and the inclusive dates of each):

____

____

10. Is your net worth (exclusive of home, furnishings, and automobiles) in excess of One Hundred Thousand ($100,000.00)

Dollars? If not, what is your net worth (exclusive of home, furnishings, and automobiles) to the nearest Ten Thousand Dollars ($10,000.00)?

11. How much (in dollars) of your income of the past two years is or do you expect to be subject to Federal Income Tax at a rate of at least fifty percent (50%)?
12. What portion (in dollars), if any, of your income for the previous year was subject to Federal Income Tax at a rate of at least fifty percent (50%) (or would have been subject to such tax at a rate of fifty percent (50%) or more, if you had not invested in any tax shelters)?
13. Have you previously invested in oil and gas drilling and recovery programs within the past five (5) years? If so, please complete.

    Nature of program Amount invested

    ____

    ____

14. Have you previously invested in other tax-shelter or related investments? If so, please complete.

    ____

    ____

15. Do you intend to rely upon the advice of an attorney, accountant or other financial advisor? If yes, please identify such person(s).

The foregoing statements are true and accurate to the best of my information and belief, and I will notify XYZ OIL COMPANY, INC. about any change in the information set forth above prior to my investment.

The foregoing information is being supplied to you for the sole purpose of enabling you to confirm that my education, past business background, and investment experience and general financial standing would enable me to make an investment in the Program.

This information is to be kept strictly confidential and may be used only for the purposes specified herein.

Yours very truly,
(Signature)

Though the company may have valid reasons for requesting all of this information, it is my personal feeling that I would not wish to invest with a company which felt entitled into digging quite that deeply into my personal life. But that is an individual reaction which may not be valid for each person or under all circumstances.

APPENDIX E

Oil, gas, and mineral lease

The following is the standard form for an oil, gas, and mineral lease used in the State of Texas. Other states may have slightly different forms, but on the whole they are likely to be quite similar.

SINGLE ACKNOWLEDGMENT

THE STATE OF TEXAS, }
COUNTY OF }

BEFORE ME, the undersigned, a Notary Public in and for said County and State, on this day personally appeared

known to me to be the person whose name subscribed to the foregoing instrument, and acknowledged to me that he executed the same for the purposes and consideration therein expressed.

GIVEN UNDER MY HAND AND SEAL OF OFFICE this the day of A. D. 19

(L. S.) --

Notary Public in and for County, Texas

SINGLE ACKNOWLEDGMENT

THE STATE OF TEXAS, }
COUNTY OF }

BEFORE ME, the undersigned, a Notary Public in and for said County and State, on this day personally appeared

known to me to be the person whose name subscribed to the foregoing instrument, and acknowledged to me that he executed the same for the purposes and consideration therein expressed.

GIVEN UNDER MY HAND AND SEAL OF OFFICE this the day of A. D. 19

(L. S.) --

Notary Public in and for County, Texas

WIFE'S SEPARATE ACKNOWLEDGMENT

THE STATE OF TEXAS, }
COUNTY OF }

BEFORE ME, the undersigned, a Notary Public in and for said County and State, on this day personally appeared , wife of , known to me to be the person whose name is subscribed to the foregoing instrument, and having been examined by me privily and apart from her husband, and having the same fully explained to her, she, the said acknowledged such instrument to be her act and deed, and she declared that she had willingly signed the same for the purposes and consideration therein expressed, and that she did not wish to retract it.

GIVEN UNDER MY HAND AND SEAL OF OFFICE this the day of A. D. 19

(L. S.) --

Notary Public in and for County, Texas

JOINT ACKNOWLEDGMENT

THE STATE OF TEXAS, }
COUNTY OF }

BEFORE ME, the undersigned, a Notary Public in and for said County and State, on this day personally appeared and , his wife, both known to me to be the persons whose names are subscribed to the foregoing instrument, and acknowledged to me that they each executed the same for the purposes and consideration therein expressed, and the said , wife of the said having been examined by me privily and apart from her husband, and having the same fully explained to her, she, the said acknowledged such instrument to be her act and deed, and she declared that she had willingly signed the same for the purposes and consideration therein expressed, and that she did not wish to retract it.

GIVEN UNDER MY HAND AND SEAL OF OFFICE, this the day of A. D. 19

(L. S.) --

Notary Public in and for County, Texas.

PRODUCERS 88 (1-64)—TEXAS

No.______

Oil, Gas and Mineral Lease

FROM

TO

Dated______, 19

No. Acres______County, Texas

Term

This instrument was filed for record on the

day of______19____, at

o'clock______M., and duly

Recorded in Book______, Page

of the______records of this office.

County Clerk

______County, Texas

By______, Deputy

When recorded return to

Texas Standard Form

Producers 88 Revised 1-64—Texas

OIL, GAS AND MINERAL LEASE

THIS AGREEMENT made this .... day of .... 19....., between

____

____

Lessor (whether one or more) and ....
Lessee, WITNESSETH:

1. Lessor in consideration of .... Dollars

($ ....) in hand paid, of the royalties herein provided, and of the agreements of Lessee herein contained, hereby grants, leases and lets exclusively unto Lessee for the purpose of investigating, exploring, prospecting, drilling and mining for and producing oil, gas and all other minerals, laying pipe lines, building tanks, power stations, telephone lines and other structures thereon to produce save, take care of, treat, transport, and own said products,

and housing its employees, the following described land in .... County Texas to-wit:

and containing .... acres, more or less. In the event a resurvey of said lands shall reveal the existence of excess and/or vacant lands lying adjacent to the lands above described and the lessor, his heirs, or assigns, shall, by virtue of his ownership of the lands above described, have preference right to acquire said excess and/or vacant lands, then in that event this lease shall cover and include all such excess and/or vacant lands which the lessor, his heirs, or assigns, shall have the preference right to acquire by virtue of his ownership of the lands above described as and when acquired by the lessor; and the lessee shall pay the lessor for such excess and/or vacant lands at the same rate per acre as the cash consideration paid for the acreage hereinabove mentioned.

2. Subject to the other provisions herein contained, this lease shall be for a term of ___ years from this date (called "primary term") and as long thereafter as oil, gas or other mineral is produced from said land hereunder.

3. The Royalties to be paid Lessor are: (a) on oil, one-eighth of that produced and saved from said land, the same to be delivered at the wells or to the credit of Lessor into the pipe line to which the wells may be connected. Lessee may from time to time purchase any royalty oil in its possession, paying the market price therefor prevailing for the field where produced on the date of purchase; (b) on gas, including casinghead gas or other gaseous substances, produced from said land and sold or used off the premises or in the manufacture of gasoline or other product therefrom, the market value at the well of one-eighth of the gas so sold or used, provided that on gas sold at the wells the royalty shall be one-eighth of the amount realized from such sale; where gas from a well producing gas or gas and condensate only is not sold or used, Lessee may pay or tender as royalty, by check or draft of Lessee, to the owner of such royalty, or to their credit in the depository bank named in the lease, on or before ninety days after the date on which said well is shut in and annually thereafter, a sum equal to the amount of annual rental payable in lieu of drilling operations during the primary term of this lease on the number of acres subject to this lease at the time such payment is made, and if such payment is made it will be considered that gas is being produced within the meaning of Paragraph 2 hereof; and (c) all other minerals mined and marketed, one-tenth either in kind or value at the well or mine, at Lessee's election, except that on sulphur the royalty shall be fifty cents (50c) per long ton. Lessee shall have free use of oil, gas, coal, wood and water from said land, except water from Lessor's wells, for all operations hereunder, and the royalty on oil, gas and coal shall be computed after deducting any so used. Lessor shall have the privilege at his risk and expense of using gas from any gas well on said land for stoves and inside lights in the principal dwelling thereon out of any surplus gas not needed for operations hereunder.

4. If operations for drilling are not commenced on said land on or before one year from this date the lease shall then terminate as to both parties unless on or before such anniversary date Lessee shall pay or tender to Lessor or to credit of Lessor in

.... Bank at .... (which bank and its successors are Lessor's agent and shall continue as the depository for all rentals payable hereunder regardless of changes in ownership of said land or the rentals) the sum

of .... Dollars

($ ....), (herein called rental), which shall cover the privilege of deferring commencement of drilling operations for a period of twelve (12) months. In like manner and upon like payments or tenders annually the commencement of drilling operations may be further deferred for successive periods of twelve (12) months each during the primary term. The payment or tender of rental may be made by the check or draft of Lessee mailed or delivered to said bank on or before such date of payment. If such bank (or any successor bank) should fail, liquidate or be succeeded by another bank, or for any reason fail or refuse to accept rental, Lessee shall not be held in default for failure to make such payment or tender of rental until thirty (30) days after Lessor shall deliver to Lessee a proper recordable instrument, naming another bank as agent to receive such payments or tenders. The down cash payment is consideration for this lease according to its terms and shall not be allocated as mere rental for a period. Lessee may at any time execute and deliver to Lessor or to the depository above named or place of record a release or releases covering any portion or portions of the above described premises and thereby surrender this lease as to such portion or portions and be relieved of all obligations as to the acreage surrendered, and thereafter the rentals payable hereunder shall be reduced in the proportion that the acreage covered hereby is reduced by said release or releases. In this connection the above described premises

shall be treated as comprising.............................. acres, whether there be more or less.

5. If prior to discovery of oil or gas on said land Lessee should drill a dry hole or holes thereon, or if after discovery of oil or gas the production thereof should cease from any cause, this lease shall not terminate if Lessee commences additional drilling or re-working operations within sixty (60) days thereafter or (if it be within the primary term) commences or resumes the payment or tender of rentals on or before the rental paying date next ensuing after the expiration of three months from date of completion of dry hole or cessation of production. If at the expiration of the primary term oil, gas or other mineral is not being produced on said land but Lessee is then engaged in drilling or re-working operations thereon, the lease shall remain in force so long as operations are prosecuted with no cessation of more than thirty (30) consecutive days, and if they result in the production of oil, gas or other minerals so long thereafter as oil, gas or other mineral is produced from said land. In the event a well or wells producing oil or gas in paying quantities should be brought in on adjacent land and within six hundred sixty (660) feet of and draining the leased premises, Lessee agrees to drill such offset wells as a reasonably prudent operator would drill under the same or similar circumstances.

6. Lessee shall have the right at any time during or after the expiration of this lease to remove all property and fixtures placed by Lessee on said land, including the right to draw and remove all casing. When required by Lessor, Lessee will bury all pipe lines below ordinary plow depth, and no well shall be drilled within two hundred (200) feet of any residence or barn now on said land without Lessor's consent.

7. The rights of either party hereunder may be assigned in whole or in part and the provisions hereof shall extend to the heirs, successors and assigns, but no change or divisions in ownership of the land, rentals, or royalties, however accomplished, shall operate to enlarge the obligations or diminish the rights of Lessee. No sale or assignment by Lessor shall be binding on Lessee until Lessee shall be furnished with a certified copy of recorded instrument evidencing same. In event of assignment of this lease as to a segregated portion of said land, the rentals payable hereunder shall be apportionable as between the several leasehold owners ratably according to the surface area of each, and default in rental payment by one shall not affect the rights of other leasehold owners hereunder.

8. The breach by Lessee of any obligation arising hereunder shall not work a forfeiture or termination of this lease nor cause a termination or reversion of the estate created hereby nor be grounds for cancellation hereof in whole or in part save as herein expressly provided. If the obligation for reasonable development should require the drilling of a well or wells, Lessee shall have ninety (90) days after ultimate judicial ascertainment of the existence of such obligation within which to begin the drilling of a well, and the only penalty for failure to do so shall be the termination of this lease save as to forty (40) acres for each well being worked on and/or being drilled and/or producing oil or gas to be selected by Lessee so that each 40-acre tract will embrace one such well.

9. Lessor hereby warrants and agrees to defend the title to said land and agrees that Lessee at its option may discharge any tax, mortgage or other lien upon said land and in event Lessee does so, it shall be subrogated to such lien with the right to enforce same and apply rentals and royalties accruing hereunder toward satisfying same. Without impairment of Lessee's rights under the warranty in event of failure of title, it is agreed that if Lessor owns an interest in said land less than the entire fee simple estate, then the royalties and rentals to be paid Lessor shall be reduced proportionately.

10. If any operation permitted or required hereunder, or the performance by Lessee of any covenant, agreement, or requirement hereof is delayed or interrupted directly or indirectly by any past or future acts, orders, regulations or requirements of the Government of the United States or any state or other governmental body, or any agency, officer, representative or authority of any of them, or because of delay or inability to get materials, labor, equipment or supplies, or on account of any other similar or dissimilar cause beyond the control of Lessee, the period of such delay or interruption shall not be counted against the Lessee, and the primary term of this lease shall automatically be extended after the expiration of the primary term set forth in Section 2 above, so long as the cause or causes for such delays or interruptions continue and for a period of six (6) months thereafter; and such extended term shall constitute and shall be considered for the purposes of this lease as a part of the primary term hereof. The provisions of Section 4 hereof, relating to the payment of delay rentals shall in all things be applicable to the primary term as extended hereby just as if such extended term were a part of the original primary term fixed in Section 2 hereof. The Lessee shall not be liable to Lessor in damages for failure to perform any operation permitted or required hereunder or to comply with any covenant, agreement or requirement hereof during the time Lessee is relieved from the obligations to comply with such covenants, agreements or requirement.

IN WITNESS WHEREOF, this instrument is executed on the date first above written.

WITNESSES:

APPENDIX F

Associations of independent oil and gas producers and other energy-related organizations

In virtually every area in the country, there is an association comprised of the people who are involved in oil or gas exploration activities. All the associations listed here are associated with the national umbrella organization, the Independent Petroleum Association of America. Anyone interested in getting financially or otherwise involved in the oil business would be well advised to contact one of these organizations for whatever information he or she may need.

INDEPENDENT PETROLEUM ASSOCIATION OF AMERICA
1101 Sixteenth Street, N.W.
Washington D.C. 20036 — 202 857 4722
C. John Miller, President

AMERICAN ASSOCIATION OF PETROLEUM LANDMEN
P.O. Box 1984
Fort Worth, TX 76101 — 817 335 9751
Harry L. Sprinkle, Executive Vice President

ARKOMA BASIN INDEPENDENT GAS PRODUCERS ASSOCIATION
c/o Miller Drilling Company
Route 3, Box 22X
Fort Smith, AR 72901 — 501 646 3481
Robert E. Miller, President

ASSOCIATION OF OILWELL SERVICING CONTRACTORS
6060 North Central Expressway, Suite 538
Dallas, TX 75206 214 692 0771
John T. Haggin, Executive Vice President

CALIFORNIA INDEPENDENT PRODUCERS ASSOCIATION
P.O. Box 24006
1100 Glendon, #1621
Los Angeles, CA 90024 213 477 3509
James H. Woods, Executive Vice President

EASTERN KANSAS OIL AND GAS ASSOCIATION, INC.
P.O. Box 340
Chanute, KS 66720 316 431 1020
Dwayne Dalton, Secretary

ILLINOIS OIL AND GAS ASSOCIATION
P.O. Box 788
Mt. Vernon, IL 62864 618 242 2857
Charles J. Pardee, Executive Secretary

INDEPENDENT OIL AND GAS ASSOCIATION OF WEST VIRGINIA
Room 207, Medical Arts Building
1021 Quarrier Street
Charleston, WV 25301 304 344 9867
Loutellus M. Stout, Executive Secretary

INDEPENDENT OIL PRODUCERS' AGENCY
4647 Long Beach Boulevard, Building D
Long Beach, CA 90805 213 595 4419
J. S. Gilstrap, Executive Vice President

INDEPENDENT OIL PRODUCERS TRI-STATE, INC.
116 Mulberry Street
Evansville, IN 47713 812 423 3231
Lester Cole, Executive Secretary

INDEPENDENT PETROLEUM ASSOCIATION OF THE MOUNTAIN STATES
518 17th Street, Suite 1214
Denver, CO 80202 303 623 0987
Larry Siegel, Executive Director

INDEPENDENT PETROLEUM ASSOCIATION OF NEW MEXICO
First Northern Plaza
P.O. Drawer 2529

Santa Fe, NM 87501 505 982 2500
Alvin Baca, Executive Director

INDIANA OIL AND GAS ASSOCIATION
c/o Robinson Engineering
P.O. Box 5269
Evansville, IN 47715 812 477 1575
C. A. Robinson, President

INTERNATIONAL ASSOCIATION OF DRILLING CONTRACTORS
P.O. Box 4287
Houston, TX 77210 713 784 4090
Ed McGhee, Executive Vice President

KANSAS INDEPENDENT OIL AND GAS ASSOCIATION
940 Fourth Financial Center
Wichita, KS 67202 316 263 7297
Donald P. Schnacke, Executive Vice President

KENTUCKY OIL AND GAS ASSOCIATION
218 West 8th Street
Owensboro, KY 42301 502 683 1886
Mrs. Wanda B. Tichener, Executive Secretary

LIAISON COMMITTEE OF COOPERATING OIL AND GAS ASSOCIATIONS
c/o TIPRO
1770 Austin National Bank Tower
Austin, TX 78701 512 477 4452
Julian Martin, Secretary Treasurer

LOUISIANA LANDOWNERS ASSOCIATION, INC.
P.O. Box 2174
Baton Rouge, LA 70821 504 383 4077
Will Abshire, Executive Director

LOUISIANA ASSOCIATION OF INDEPENDENT PRODUCERS AND ROYALTY OWNERS
P.O. Box 65197
Baton Rouge, LA 70896 504 926 8744
Thomas M. Barton, Executive Vice President

MICHIGAN OIL AND GAS ASSOCIATION
P.O. Box 15069
Lansing, MI 48933 517 487 1092
Frank L. Mortl, Executive Vice President

NATIONAL STRIPPER WELL ASSOCIATION
7137 South Darlington Avenue
Tulsa, OK 74136 — 918 492 2054
Clyde LaMotte, Executive Vice President

NEW MEXICO OIL AND GAS ASSOCIATION
P.O. Box 1864
Santa Fe, NM 87501 — 505 982 2568
Peter Hanagan, Executive Vice President

NEW YORK STATE OIL PRODUCERS ASSOCIATION
P.O. Box 265
Bolivar, NY 14745
William F. Hogan, Secretary-Treasurer

NORTH TEXAS OIL AND GAS ASSOCIATION
1106 City National Building
Wichita Falls, TX 76301 — 817 723 4131
Dr. Tom Haywood, Executive Vice President

OHIO OIL AND GAS ASSOCIATION
P.O. Box 1008
Newark, OH 43055 — 614 344 9448
Kirk Jordan, Executive Vice President

OKLAHOMA INDEPENDENT PETROLEUM ASSOCIATION
124 East 4th Street
Tulsa, OK 74103 — 913 584 1233
Steven R. Kelley, Executive Director

PANHANDLE PRODUCERS AND ROYALTY OWNERS ASSOCIATION
701 Bank of the Southwest Building
Amarillo, TX 79109 — 806 352 5637
B. D. King, Executive Vice President

PENNSYLVANIA GRADE CRUDE OIL ASSOCIATION
c/o K-Arcy Corporation
313 North Main Street
Wellsville, NY 14895 — 716 593 1799
K. R. Cochran, President

PENNSYLVANIA OIL AND GAS ASSOCIATION
P.O. Drawer D
Custer City, PA 16725 — 814 368 6222
E. James Bryner, President

PERMIAN BASIN PETROLEUM ASSOCIATION
P.O. Box 132
Midland, TX 79702 915 684 6345
James E. Thompson, Executive Vice President

ROCKY MOUNTAIN OIL AND GAS ASSOCIATION
345 Petroleum Club Building
Denver, CO 80202 303 534 8261
Jack Swenson, Executive Vice President

TENNESSEE OIL AND GAS ASSOCIATION
5711 Old Harding Road
Nashville, TN 37205 615 352 0499
Bill Goodwin, Executive Vice President

TEXAS INDEPENDENT PRODUCERS AND ROYALTY OWNERS ASSOCIATION
1770 Austin National Bank Tower
Austin, TX 78701 512 477 4452
W. Earl Turner, Executive Vice President

VIRGINIA OIL AND GAS ASSOCIATION
P.O. Box 1837
Wise, VA 24293
Reo F. Ford, President

WEST CENTRAL TEXAS OIL AND GAS ASSOCIATION
P.O. Box 2332
Abilene, TX 79604 915 677 2469
Glen Michel, Executive Vice President

DEPARTMENT OF COMMERCE
14th and Constitution Avenues, N.W.
Washington, D.C. 20241

DEPARTMENT OF ENERGY
1000 Independent Avenue S.W.
Washington, D.C. 20545

DEPARTMENT OF THE INTERIOR
18th and C Streets N.W.
Washington, D.C. 20240

DEPARTMENT OF TRANSPORTATION
400 7th Street S.W.
Washington, D.C. 20590

ENVIRONMENTAL PROTECTION AGENCY
401 M Street N.W.
Washington, D.C. 20460

FEDERAL ENERGY REGULATORY COMMISSION
825 North Capitol Street N.E.
Washington, D.C. 20426

U.S. GEOLOGICAL SURVEY
National Center
Sunrise Valley Drive
Reston, VA 22092

INTERSTATE COMMERCE COMMISSION
12th and Constitution Avenue N.W.
Washington, D.C. 20423

ABILENE GEOLOGICAL SOCIETY
Box 974
Abilene, TX 79604

ALABAMA NATURAL GAS ASSOCIATION
2301 First National-Southern Natural Building
Box 785
Birmingham, AL 35201

ALASKA GEOLOGICAL SOCIETY, INC.
P.O. Box 1288
Anchorage, AK 99510

ALASKA OIL AND GAS CONSERVATION COMMITTEE
3001 Porcupine Drive
Anchorage, AK 99501

AMERICAN ASSOCIATION OF PETROLEUM GEOLOGISTS
Box 979
Tulsa, OK 74101

AMERICAN ASSOCIATION OF PETROLEUM LANDMEN
P.O. Box 1984
Fort Worth, TX 76101

AMERICAN GAS ASSOCIATION
1515 Wilson Boulevard
Arlington, VA 22209

AMERICAN GEOLOGICAL INSTITUTE
5205 Leesburg Drive
Falls Church, VA 22041

AMERICAN GEOPHYSICAL UNION
1909 K Street N.W.
Washington, D.C. 20006

AMERICAN INSTITUTE OF MINING, METALLURGY, AND PETROLEUM ENGINEERS
United Engineering Center
345 East 47th Street
New York, NY 10017

AMERICAN INSTITUTE OF PROFESSIONAL GEOLOGISTS
P.O. Box 957
Boulder, CO 80401

AMERICAN PETROLEUM INSTITUTE
2101 L Street N.W.
Washington, D.C. 20037

AMERICAN PETROLEUM REFINERS ASSOCIATION
18th and M Streets N.W.
Washington, D.C. 20036

AMERICAN SOCIETY OF MECHANICAL ENGINEERS
United Engineering Center
345 East 47th Street
New York, NY 10017

APPALACHIAN GEOLOGICAL SOCIETY
P.O. Box 2605
Charleston, WV 25329

ARDMORE GEOLOGICAL SOCIETY
P.O. Box 1552
Ardmore, OK 73401

ARIZONA OIL AND GAS CONSERVATION COMMISSION
1645 West Jefferson, Suite 420
Phoenix, AZ 85007

ARKANSAS OIL AND GAS COMMISSION
314 East Oak Street
El Dorado, AR 71730

ASPHALT INSTITUTE
Asphalt Institute Building
College Park, MD 20740

ASSOCIATION OF OIL PIPE LINES
1725 K Street, Suite 1208
Washington, D.C. 20006

ASSOCIATION OF OIL WELL SERVICING CONTRACTORS
6060 North Central Expressway, Suite 462
Dallas, TX 75206

ASSOCIATION OF PETROLEUM RE-REFINERS
1101 Connecticut Avenue N.W., Suite 700
Washington, D.C. 20036

BUREAU OF GEOLOGY
Division of Resource Management
Florida Department of Natural Resources
903 West Tennessee Street
Tallahassee, FL 32304

CALIFORNIA DEPARTMENT OF CONSERVATION, OIL AND GAS DIVISION
1416 Ninth Street, Room 1316
Sacramento, CA 95814

CALIFORNIA GAS PRODUCERS ASSOCIATION
626 Wilshire Boulevard
Los Angeles, CA 90024

COLORADO OIL AND GAS CONSERVATION COMMISSION
1313 Sherman Street, Room 721
Denver, CO 80203

CONSERVATION COMMITTEE OF CALIFORNIA OIL PRODUCERS
417 South Hill Street, Room 868
Los Angeles, CA 90013

CORPUS CHRISTI GEOLOGICAL SOCIETY
P.O. Box 1068
Corpus Christi, TX 78403

DALLAS GEOLOGICAL SOCIETY
One Energy Square, Suite 100
Dallas, TX 75206

DEPARTMENT OF CONSERVATION AND NATURAL RESOURCES
Division of Mineral Resources
201 South Fall Street, Capitol Complex
Carson, NV 89701

DEPARTMENT OF NATURAL RESOURCES
P.O. Box 44396, Capitol Station
Baton Rouge, LA 70804

EAST TEXAS GEOLOGICAL SOCIETY
P.O. Box 216
Tyler, TX 75710

FLORIDA NATURAL GAS ASSOCIATION
815 Briercliff Drive
Orlando, FL 32806

FORT WORTH GEOLOGICAL SOCIETY
c/o John Breyer
Texas Christian University
Fort Worth, TX 76129

FOUR CORNERS GEOLOGICAL SOCIETY
P.O. Box 1501
Durango, CO 81301

GAS PROCESSORS ASSOCIATION
1812 First Place
Tulsa, OK 74103

GAS RESEARCH INSTITUTE
10 West 35th Street
Chicago, IL 60616

GEOLOGICAL SOCIETY OF AMERICA
3300 Penrose Place
Boulder, CO 80301

GEOLOGICAL SOCIETY OF KENTUCKY
600 Federal Place, Room 572
Louisville, KY 40202

HOUSTON GEOLOGICAL SOCIETY
806 Main Street, Suite B-1
Houston, TX 77002

IDAHO OIL AND GAS CONSERVATION COMMISSION
Department of Lands
State Capitol Building
Boise, ID 83720

ILLINOIS DEPARTMENT OF MINES AND MINERALS
704 William G. Stratton Building
Springfield, IL 62706

ILLINOIS GEOLOGICAL SOCIETY
Department of Earth Sciences
Southern Illinois University
Edwardsville, IL 62025

ILLINOIS GEOLOGICAL SURVEY
Natural Resources Boulding
Urbana, IL 61801

INDEPENDENT REFINERS ASSOCIATION OF AMERICA
1220 19th Street N.W., Suite 403
Washington, D.C. 20036

INDEPENDENT REFINERS ASSOCIATION OF CALIFORNIA
900 Wilshire Boulevard, Suite 736
Los Angeles, CA 90017

INDEPENDENT TERMINAL OPERATORS ASSOCIATION
1523 L Street NW
Washington, D.C. 20005

INDIANA DEPARTMENT OF NATURAL RESOURCES
Division of Oil and Gas
911 State Office Building
Indianapolis, IN 46204

INDIANA GEOLOGICAL SURVEY
Department of Natural Resources
611 North Walnut Grove
Bloomington, IN 47401

INDIANA OIL MARKETERS ASSOCIATION
8780 Purdue Road, Suite 4
Indianapolis, IN 46268

INSTITUTE OF GAS TECHNOLOGY
3424 South State Street
Chicago, IL 60616

INSTRUMENT SOCIETY OF AMERICA
400 Stanwix Street
Pittsburgh, PA 15222

INTERNATIONAL ASSOCIATION OF GEOPHYSICAL CONTRACTORS
7207 Regency Square Boulevard, Suite 140
Houston. TX 77036

INTERNATIONAL OIL SCOUTS ASSOCIATION
P.O. Box 2121
Austin, TX 78768

INTERSTATE NATURAL GAS ASSOCIATION OF AMERICA
1660 L Street N.W.
Washington, D.C. 20036

INTERSTATE OIL COMPACT COMMISSION
P.O. Box 53127
Oklahoma City, OK 73152

IOWA GEOLOGICAL SURVEY
123 North Capitol Street
Iowa City, IA 52242

KANSAS CORPORATION COMMISSION
Oil and Gas Conservation Division
245 North Water Street
Wichita, KS 67202

KANSAS GEOLOGICAL SOCIETY
304 Insurance Building
Wichita, KS 67202

KANSAS GEOLOGICAL SURVEY
University of Kansas
1930 Avenue A, Campus West
Lawrence, KS 66044

KENTUCKY DEPARTMENT OF MINES AND MINERALS
Oil and Gas Division
P.O. Box 680
Lexington, KY 40586

KENTUCKY OIL AND GAS ASSOCIATION
218 West 8th Street
Owensboro, KY 42301

LAFAYETTE GEOLOGICAL SOCIETY
P.O. Box 51896
Lafayette, LA 70505

LIBERAL GEOLOGICAL SOCIETY
P.O. Box 902
Liberal, KS 67901

LOS ANGELES BASIN GEOLOGICAL SOCIETY
P.O. Box 1072
Bakersfield, CA 93302

LOUISIANA GEOLOGICAL SURVEY
P.O. Box G, University Station
Baton Rouge, LA 70821

LOUISIANA OFFICE OF CONSERVATION
P.O. Box 44275, 625 North 4th Street
Baton Rouge, LA 70804

MARYLAND GEOLOGICAL SURVEY
Merryman Hall, Johns Hopkins University
Baltimore, MD 21218

MICHIGAN BASIN GEOLOGICAL SOCIETY
Michigan Department of Natural Resources
Geological Survey Division
P.O. Box 30028
Lansing, MI 48909

MICHIGAN DEPARTMENT OF NATURAL RESOURCES
Stevens T. Mason Building
Lansing, MI 48926

MICHIGAN GEOLOGICAL SURVEY
P.O. Box 30028
Lansing, MI 48909

MICHIGAN PETROLEUM ASSOCIATION
400 Michigan National Tower
Lansing, MI 48933

MID-CONTINENT OIL AND GAS ASSOCIATION
1111 Thompson Building
Tulsa, OK 74103

MIDWEST GAS ASSOCIATION, INC.
7300 France Avenue South, Suite 322
Minneapolis, MN 55435

MISSISSIPPI GEOLOGICAL, ECONOMIC AND TOPOGRAPHICAL SURVEY
P.O. Box 4915, 2525 North West Street
Jackson, MS 39216

MISSISSIPPI GEOLOGICAL SOCIETY
P.O. Box 422
Jackson, MS 39205

MISSISSIPPI STATE OIL AND GAS BOARD
P.O. Box 1332
Jackson, MS 39205

MISSOURI OIL AND GAS COUNCIL
P.O. Box 250
Rolla, MO 65401

MONTANA BUREAU OF MINES AND GEOLOGY
Montana College of Mineral Science and Technology
Butte, MT 59701

MONTANA DEPARTMENT OF NATURAL RESOURCES AND CONSERVATION
Board of Oil and Gas Conservation
P.O. Box 217
Helena, MT 59601

MONTANA GEOLOGICAL SOCIETY
P.O. Box 844
Billings, MT 59103

NATIONAL ASSOCIATION OF CORROSION ENGINEERS
1440 South Creek
Houston, TX 77084

NATIONAL LP-GAS ASSOCIATION
1301 West 22nd Street
Oak Brook, IL 60521

NATIONAL PETROLEUM REFINERS ASSOCIATION
1899 L Street, NW, Suite 100
Washington, D.C. 20036

NEBRASKA OIL AND GAS CONSERVATION COMMISSION
P.O. Box 399
Sidney, NB 69162

NEW MEXICO GEOLOGICAL SOCIETY, INC.
Campus Station
Socorro, NM 87801

NEW MEXICO OIL CONSERVATION COMMISSION
P.O. Box 2088
Santa Fe, NM 87501

NEW ORLEANS GEOLOGICAL SOCIETY, INC.
P.O. Box 52172
New Orleans, LA 70152

NEW YORK STATE DEPARTMENT OF ENVIRONMENTAL CONSERVATION
50 Wolf Road
Albany, NY 12233

NEW YORK STATE GEOLOGICAL ASSOCIATION
Department of Geological Sciences, Hofstra University
Hempstead, NY 11550

NORTH CAROLINA DEPARTMENT OF NATURAL RESOURCES
P.O. Box 27687
Raleigh, NC 27611

NORTH DAKOTA GEOLOGICAL SOCIETY
P.O. Box 82
Bismarck, ND 58501

NORTH DAKOTA GEOLOGICAL SURVEY
University Station
Grand Forks, ND 58202

NORTHERN CALIFORNIA GEOLOGICAL SOCIETY
California Division of Mines and Geology
Ferry Building
San Francisco, CA 94111

NORTH TEXAS GEOLOGICAL SOCIETY
P.O. Box 1671
Wichita Falls, TX 76301

OFFICE OF MINERAL RESOURCES, STATE MINERAL BOARD
P.O. Drawer 2827
Baton Rouge, LA 70821

OHIO DEPARTMENT OF NATURAL RESOURCES
Division of Oil and Gas
Fountain Square, Building B
Columbus, OH 43224

OHIO GEOLOGICAL SOCIETY
P.O. Box 14322, Beechwood Station
Columbus, OH 43214

OHIO OIL AND GAS ASSOCIATION
P.O. Box 1008
Newark, OH 43055

OKLAHOMA CITY GEOLOGICAL SOCIETY, INC.
1020 First Life Assurance Building
Oklahoma City, OK 73102

OKLAHOMA CORPORATION COMMISSION
Oil and Gas Conservation Division
Jim Thorpe Building
Oklahoma City, OK 73105

OKLAHOMA GEOLOGICAL SURVEY
University of Oklahoma
830 Van Vleet Oval, Room 163
Norman, OK 73019

OKLAHOMA OIL MARKETERS ASSOCIATION
5115 North Western
Oklahoma City, OK 73118

OREGON DEPARTMENT OF GEOLOGY AND MINERAL INDUSTRIES
1069 State Office Building
Portland, OR 97201

PACIFIC COAST GAS ASSOCIATION, INC.
1650 South Amphlett Boulevard
San Mateo, CA 94402

PACIFIC ENERGY ASSOCIATION
3050 Daimler Avenue
Santa Ana, CA 92705

PANHANDLE GEOLOGICAL SOCIETY
P.O. Box 2473
Amarillo, TX 79105

PENNSYLVANIA DEPARTMENT OF ENVIRONMENTAL RESOURCES
P.O. Box 2063
Harrisburg, PA 17120

PENNSYLVANIA GRADE CRUDE OIL ASSOCIATION
P.O. Box 250
Oil City, PA 16301

PENNSYLVANIA PETROLEUM ASSOCIATION
Building 2, Suite D, 2101 North Front Street
Harrisburg, PA 17110

PETROLEUM EQUIPMENT INSTITUTE
P.O. Box 2380
Tulsa, OK 74101

PETROLEUM EQUIPMENT SUPPLIERS ASSOCIATION
9225 Katy Freeway, Suite 401
Houston, TX 77024

PETROLEUM EXPLORATION SOCIETY OF NEW YORK
P.O. Box 3443, Grand Central Station
New York, NY 10017

PIPELINE CONTRACTORS ASSOCIATION
2800 Republic National Bank Building
Dallas, TX 75201

SAN ANGELO GEOLOGICAL SOCIETY
P.O. Box 1668
San Angelo, TX 76902

SAN JOAQUIN GEOLOGICAL SOCIETY
P.O. Box 1056
Bakersfield, CA 93302

SOCIETY OF EXPLORATION GEOPHYSICISTS
P.O. Box 3098
Tulsa, OK 74101

SOCIETY OF INDEPENDENT PROFESSIONAL EARTH SCIENTISTS
P.O. Box 3370
Midland, TX 79702

SOCIETY OF PETROLEUM ENGINEERS
6200 North Central Expressway
Dallas, TX 75206

SOCIETY OF PROFESSIONAL WELL LOG ANALYSTS
806 Main Street, Suite B-1
Houston, TX 77001

SOUTH CAROLINA GEOLOGICAL SOCIETY
Habison Forest Road
Columbia, SC 29210

SOUTH DAKOTA GEOLOGICAL SURVEY
Science Center, University of South Dakota
Vermillion, SD 57069

SOUTH DAKOTA INDEPENDENT OIL MEN'S ASSOCIATION
P.O. Box 1058
Pierre, SD 57501

SOUTHEASTERN GEOLOGICAL SOCIETY
P.O. Box 1634
Tallahassee, FL 32302

SOUTHERN GAS ASSOCIATION
4230 LBJ Freeway, Suite 414
Dallas, TX 75234

SOUTH TEXAS GEOLOGICAL SOCIETY
B-100 Petroleum Center
San Antonio, TX 78209

SOUTHWEST KANSAS ROYALTY OWNERS ASSOCIATION
209 East 6th Street
P.O. Box 250
Hugoton, KS 67951

SPILL CONTROL ASSOCIATION OF AMERICA
17117 West 9 Mile Road, Suite 1515
Southfield, MI 48075

STATE OIL AND GAS BOARD OF ALABAMA
P.O. Drawer O
University, AL 35486

TENNESSEE DEPARTMENT OF CONSERVATION
2611 West End Avenue
Nashville, TN 37203

TENNESSEE OIL AND GAS ASSOCIATION
5711 Old Harding Road
Nashville, TN 37205

TENNESSEE OIL MARKETERS ASSOCIATION
430 Enos Reed Drive
P.O. Box 23256
Nashville, TN 37303

TEXAS MID-CONTINENT OIL AND GAS ASSOCIATION
1341 West Mockingbird Lane, Suite 1111-E
Dallas, TX 75247

TEXAS RAILROAD COMMISSION
P.O. Drawer 12967
Austin, TX 78711

UTAH DIVISION OF OIL, GAS AND MINING
1588 West North Temple
Salt Lake City, UT 84116

UTAH GEOLOGICAL AND MINERAL SURVEY
606 Black Hawk Way, Research Center
Salt Lake City, UT 84108

UTAH GEOLOGICAL ASSOCIATION
P.O. Box 11334
Salt Lake City, UT 84147

WASHINGTON OIL AND GAS CONSERVATION COMMITTEE
Public Lands Building
Olympia, WA 98504

WESTERN OIL AND GAS ASSOCIATION
Roosevelt Building, Suite 850; 727 West 7th Street
Los Angeles, CA 90017

WEST VIRGINIA DEPARTMENT OF MINES
Oil and Gas Division
1613 Washington Street, East
Charleston, WV 25311

WEST VIRGINIA GEOLOGICAL AND ECONOMIC SURVEY
P.O. Box 879
Morgantown, WV 26505

WEST VIRGINIA OIL AND NATURAL GAS ASSOCIATION
P.O. Box 3231
Charleston, WV 25332

WEST TEXAS GEOLOGICAL SOCIETY
P.O. Box 1595
Midland, TX 79702

WYOMING GEOLOGICAL ASSOCIATION
P.O. Box 545
Casper, WY 82602

WYOMING OIL AND GAS CONSERVATION COMMISSION
Wyoming Building, P.O. Box 2640
Casper, WY 82602

Glossary

A

abd, abnd—abandoned.

acid fracture—the treatment of an existing well, using various chemicals, designed to improve the permeability of the oil-bearing formations.

acid treatment or acidize—treating limestone or dolomitic formations with chemicals designed to enlarge open spaces for increasing production.

anticline—an elongated upwarped rock structure (dome or arch).

arenaceous—sandy.

argillaceous—a nonproductive formation containing shale or clay and lacking permeability.

arkose—granite wash; granite fragments producing a sandy formation of sediment.

asphaltic—saturation composed of a mixture of solid and viscous hydrocarbons.

B

B/—bottom of (well, hole, etc.).

bail—a hollow steel cylinder containing a dump valve which is run inside the casing on a wire for recovering fluids or other material.

bail—the action described above.

basement—the undrillable rock at the bottom of the sedimentary rock structure.

basin—a region with a history of subsidence; a thick sedimentary section.

bbl—barrels (plural).

b/d—barrels per day.

bedding—the layering of rock strata; thin bedded, thick bedded, massive bedded, etc.

BFPH—barrels of fluid per hour.

BHP—bottom-hole pressure.

bioherm—a small limestone mass.

bl—black.

bld—bailed.

bleeding—oil or gas seeping through pore spaces or fractures.

blowout—the eruption of oil or gas out of a well as a result of excessive downhole pressure.

BO—barrels of oil.

bonus—the lease payment per acre for an agreed-upon period of time made to the lessor in addition to his royalty.

BOPD—barrels of oil per day.
bottom-hole contribution—a payment which may be due under the terms of an agreement between an operator and a supporting company, payable to the operator upon reaching the agreed-upon depth, regardless of whether the drilling operation resulted in a well or a dry hole.
bottom-hole pressure—the pressure found in an oil or gas-bearing reservoir.
BPD—barrels per day.
Bradenhead—the connection at the top of the oil-well casing.
breccia—rock fragments associated with a fault zone.
brkn—broken.
broken—sand containing shaly layers or any group of mixed deposits.
BW—barrels of water.
BWPD—barrels of water per day.
BWPH—barrels of water per hour.

C

cable-tool drilling—drilling with a cylindrical bit of solid steel activated by a walking beam and steel line, working vertically in the hole.
calcareous—a composition of lime minerals.
cap rock—a nonporous formation above a reservoir, preventing the upward movement of oil.
carried interest—revisionary interest; a working-interest participation in a producing well which involves reimbursement of the operator for his investment out of production before other participants begin to share in the revenue.
casing—the pipe which is cemented in the hole, such as surface casing, production casing, etc.
CFG—cubic feet of gas.
CFGPD—cubic feet of gas per day.
chalk—a soft limestone, usually mixed with earth.
channel—a cavity outside the casing; the result of a poor installation and cementing job.
chert—silica; a hard, dense mineral.
chk—choke.
choke—an aperture designed to permit the measurement of oil or gas volume.
Christmas tree—a combination of pipes, valves, and gauges atop a free-flowing well, for the purpose of controlling the flow of oil or gas.
circ—circulated.
circulation—the process which cycles the drilling mud from the mud pit to the bottom of the hole and back again.
clastic—sediment, debris, consisting of small fragments.
cln—crystalline.
comp—completed; completion.
compaction—the conversion of sediment fragments into rock.

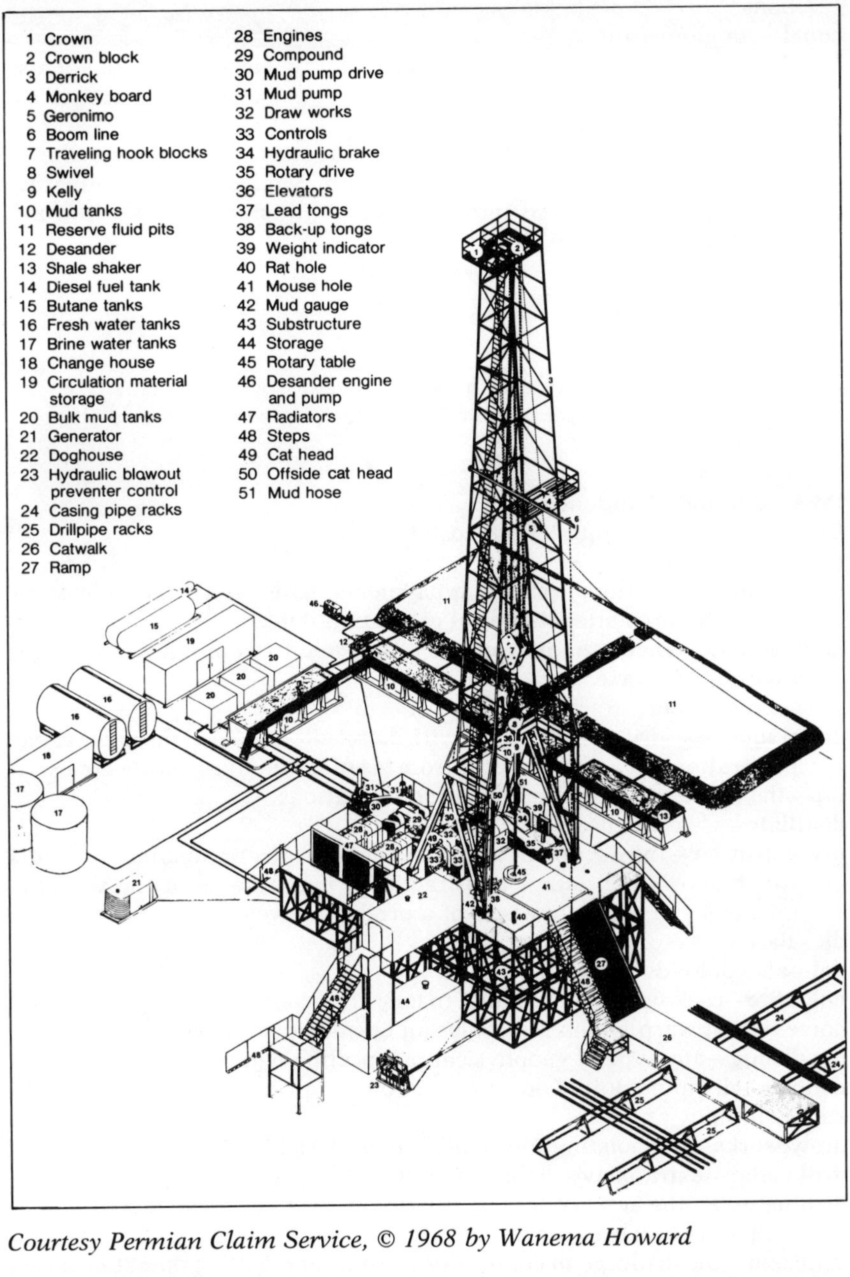

Courtesy Permian Claim Service, © 1968 by Wanema Howard

condensate—natural gasoline; a fairly colorless fluid of volatile hydrocarbons.
congl—conglomerate.
conglomerate—more or less round and partially cemented rock fragments.
coning—water entering the well as a result of damage usually caused by negligence in the production process.
core—a cylindrical section of the strata being drilled and recovered in a hollow steel container. Cores can be examined for traces of minerals.
core gun—a device lowered into the hole to fire small charges into the formations for obtaining core samples.
CP—casing pressure.
crd—cored.
crg—coring.
crude—unrefined oil.
crystalline—description of the shape and size of rock crystals.
cuttings—fragments of rock and other material resulting from drilling.

D

D&A—dry and abandoned.
D&C—drilling and completion (costs).
DC—drill collar.
delay rental—additional premium payments made on a mineral lease to keep it in force after its initial expiration date.
depletion alowance—the percentage of revenue from oil or gas which is exempt from taxes.
DF—derrick floor.
diesel squeeze—dry cement mixed with diesel oil is pumped through casing perforations to prevent water from seeping into oil-bearing zones.
dip—the angle and direction of tilting formations.
distillate—*see* condensate.
division order—the document issued by the marketer or pipeline company which shows the names and fractional participants of the working interests and royalty owners of a producing well.
dk—dark.
dol—also dolo; dolomite.
dolomite—rock with considerable magnesium content.
dome—an upwarp which resembles an upside-down bowl.
doodlebug—any type of geophysical prospecting equipment.
doubles—drillpipe pulled out, two sections at a time.
DP—drillpipe.
draw works—the hoisting mechanism in a derrick.
drill collar—extra-heavy drillstem, adding rigidity and weight.
drilling unit—the acreage leased, usually at least 40 acres, in connection with a drilling program.
drillstem—the drillpipe in connection with rotary drilling operations; the solid shaft in cable-tool drilling operations to which the drill bit is attached.

drillstem test—a procedure in which fluids or gas are released into a perforated pipe attached to the drillpipe in order to measure pressures and flow capacity.
drlg—drilling.
dry gas—gas devoid of liquid components.
dry hole—the result of a drilling project which produced neither oil nor gas nor any other marketable minerals.
dry-hole contribution—an amount paid, usually based on the number of feet drilled in a test well, when it turns out to be a dry hole.
DST—drillstem test.
duck's nest—a standby truck or pit holding extra drilling mud.
duster—dry hole.

E

elec log—electric log.
electric log—*see* log, logging.
elev—elevation.
elevation—the altitude above mean sea level at either the drilling location, the derrick floor, or the top of the bushing from which the depth of the hole is measured.
emulsion—mixture of oil, water, and mud.
est—estimated.

F

facies—short for lithofacies; rock-type development of lateral variation.
farmout—leasehold acreage, usually provided by a major oil company, to an independent operator under certain predetermined financial considerations.
fault—a zone of fracture; one side is referred to as upthrown, the other as downthrown.
FIH—fluid in hole.
fireflooding—an oil-air mixture ignited underground, breaking and thinning nearby oil and providing the needed pressure to move it to nearby producing wells.
fishing—recovering tools, cable, or pipe lost in the hole.
fl/—flowed, flowing.
flooding—injecting water into a depleted well to force oil to other wells for production.
fluor—fluorescence.
fluorescence—the property of oil and certain other minerals to glow under ultraviolet light.
fm—formation.
folding—the warping of rock formations due to movement in the earth's crust.
fourbles—drillpipe being pulled out of the hole, four sections at a time.
FP—flowing pressure.
frac—fractured; to fracture.

G

G&OCM—gas and oil-cut mud.

gas cut—gas-bearing drilling fluids which appear in the mud stream or show up during testing.

gas-oil ratio—gas in cubic feet relative to a barrel of oil.

gas repressuring—a method of thinning residual oil and moving it under pressure to certain producing wells.

gasser—a gas well.

GC—gas cut.

GCM—gas-cut mud.

general partner—the actual operator of a drilling program.

geophone—an instrument used to detect seismic signals.

GL—ground level.

GOR—gas-oil ratio.

gr—gray.

graben—a downthrown portion of a fault, located between higher formations.

granite—igneous rock, light in color, found primarily beneath oil-bearing sediments.

granite wash—*see* arkose.

gravimeter—an instrument capable of measuring variations in the earth's gravitational field. Gravity meter.

grn—green.

H

half sole—repair of a corroded section of a pipeline.

HGOR—high gas-oil ratio.

high—uppermost part of an inclined geological structure.

HOCM—heavily oil-cut mud.

horst—the upthrown portion within a fault system.

hot footing—installing a heater at the bottom of an input well to thin heavy crude oil and increase its flow to adjacant wells.

hydrocarbon—various combinations of hydrogen and carbon.

I

IDC—intangible drilling and development costs.

ig—igneous.

input well—a well drilled to force oil into adjacant producing wells.

interstitial—void spaces in the reservoir rock, often filled with water.

IP—initial production.

isopach map—a map showing the thicknesses of various formations.

J

jars—steel links in a string of drilling tools which act as buffers against sudden jerks.

joint—a length of drillpipe or casing.

jug—geophone.

K

karst—irregular surface in limestone terrain.
KB—kelly bushing.
kelly—a 40-foot square hollow stem attached to the drillpipe and turned by the rotary table.
KO—kicked off.

L

lagoonal—quiet shallow water.
lenticular—a lense-shaped formation.
lessee—the purchaser of a lease.
lessor—the person from whom a lease is purchased.
light ends—volatile products of refining such as gasoline, propane, butane.
limestone—a sedimentary rock, primarily composed of calcium carbonate.
limited partner—the investor in a drilling project who depends on the operator (general partner) to undertake the actual drilling or cause it to be undertaken.
lithofacies—*see* facies.
lithology—the science of rocks and mineral masses.
lm—lime.
load oil—oil used in treating mud or input wells.
loc—location.
log, logging—a system of determining the potential of a well, and the record kept of what has been determined, usually in the form of squiggly lines on a strip of graph paper.
lost circulation—*see* circulation.
ls—limestone.
lse—lease.

M

MCF—thousand cubic feet (of gas).
md—millidarcies.
MICT—moving in cable tools.
millidarcy—a unit of measurement of the permeability of a reservoir.
mineral rights—ownership of oil gas and other minerals beneath the surface of the earth.
MIR—moving in rig.
MMCF—million cubic feet (of gas).
MO—moving out.
mud—mixture of mud and chemicals used as lubricant in drilling operations.
mud acid—a detergent used to dissolve clay particles.

N

nitroglycerine treatment—a system used to enlarge the area of effective drainage from a reservoir.
nonoperator—limited partner.

nonparticipating royalty—ownership of mineral rights limited by time or productivity.
NS—no show.

O

O&G—oil and gas.
O&GCM—oil and gas-cut mud.
O&SW—oil and salt water.
OF—open flow.
offset—drilling a well adjacant to another according to a certain pattern. It allows for four close-in offset locations and four more distant diagonal offsets.
OH—open hole.
oil and gas lease—a contract conveying the mineral rights to given acreage for the purpose of drilling and production.
oil-base mud—drilling mud with particles suspended in the oil.
oil cut—a mixture of drilling mud and oil which is recovered during testing.
oil payment—revenue from production.
onlap, overlap—loss of a section in a marine sequence.
oolitic—formation consisting of small, rounded limestone pellets.
OPEC—Organization of Petroleum Exporting Countries.
open-hole completion—the hole is drilled deeper after casing has been cemented in place to a level above the reservoir.
operator—the person or company putting together a drilling program.
outcrop—rock formations visible at the surface.
overriding royalty—a royalty percentage over and above the usual one-eighth (12.5%) paid to the holders of the mineral rights and deducted from the revenue of the holders of the working interest.

P

packer—a rubber cylinder which is expanded against the walls of the hole or casing during drillstem tests.
paleogeologic map—pattern of ancient outcrops at areas of buried erosion.
P&A—plugged and abandoned.
PB—plugged back.
peneplane—gently sloping surface.
perforate—penetrating the casing with holes made with a perforation gun.
perforation gun—equipment used to perforate the casing at a well at a given level.
perm—permeability.
permeability—the porosity of a given formation providing oil with the ability to flow.
piercement—a salt plug penetrating rock formations to shallow depths.
pig—a cylindrical scraper used to clean the inside of a pipeline.
pits—shallow excavations used to store drilling mud or waste crude.
PL—pipeline.

plug—to plug a well by installing a solid cement plug inside the casing or capping a well with a metal plate.
plug back—plugging the lower section of the casing in order to prevent fluids from rising while a higher section is being tested.
polymerization—the formation of hydrocarbon compounds during a chemical process.
por—porosity, porous.
porosity—the condition of a formation which permits oil to flow.
psi—pounds per square inch; a measure of pressure.

Q

quartzite—sandstone hardened by silica.

R

range—township.
ream—to enlarge a hole by using a larger bit.
reef—lenticular limestone formation of considerable size, surrounded by formations of other substances.
reservoir—formations which contain or are thought to contain oil or gas.
resistivity—degree of porosity or the lack of it in a given formation.
revisionary interest—*see* carried interest.
rig—the derrick and related machinery.
rig time—time paid for by the operator rather than the drilling contractor.
rotary drilling—a system using rotary drillpipe and bit.
rotary table—the circular table, usually gear-driven, which rotates the drillpipe and bit.
roughneck—a person working on the floor of the derrick.
round trip—the changing of a drill bit.
royalty—the percentage of interest in a producing well due the holders of the mineral rights without any expense on their part. Usually one-eighth (12.5%).
RP—rock pressure.
RT—rotary table.
runs—the production or income from a lease, recorded on a run ticket and usually provided by the company buying the oil or gas.

S

salt dome—a usually deep-seated salt plug which may be indicative of oil prospects.
salting—placing traces of oil into a hole to give the impression that it might be a producer.
sandfrac, sand fracturing—sand of a certain grade and heavy oil forced into a formation under pressure to improve permeability.
sandstone—a formation consisting primarily of compacted sand.
SDO—shut down for orders.
SEC—Securities and Exchange Commission.

secondary recovery—any one of a number of systems by which oil remaining in a reservoir can be recovered through the use of heating, waterflooding, gas injection, etc.
seis—seismograph.
seismic—pertaining to the reflectivity of sound waves.
seismograph—the instrument used to record the refraction of sound waves.
service well—a well drilled for purposes other than the recovery of oil or gas, such as an input well.
SG—show of gas.
shale—impermeable rocks of clay and other substances.
shale oil—rocks containing oil which can be recovered by sophisticated methods of heat treating.
shale shaker—a vibrating sieve designed to remove drill cuttings from the drilling mud.
shoestring sand—a long, narrow sand formation.
show—expression used to indicate that traces of oil or gas are present in a core; detectable through the use of ultraviolet light, under a microscope, or simply by odor.
SI—shut in.
SIBHP—shut-in bottom-hole pressure.
sidewall core—small-diameter cylinders cut from rock in the wall of the hole.
siliceous—cemented with silica.
SIP—shut-in pressure.
slush pit—the pit containing the debris separated from the stream of drilling mud.
SO—show of oil.
SO&G—show of oil and gas.
SO&W—show of oil and water.
source beds—rich deposits of fossil residue.
spud—starting to drill a hole.
squeeze—the cementing of the back of the casing under high pressure to block off nonproductive formations.
SSO—slight show of oil.
S/T—sample tops.
stands—connected joints of drillpipe.
stratigraphic—pertaining to the age, character, and thickness of rock formations.
strike—the direction of a tilted formation.
stripper well—a well producing less than 10 barrels of oil a day.
structural trap—a fault or other geological barrier to the movement of oil.
structure—a geological term pertaining to rock formations.
sul wtr—sulphur water.
sur—survey.
SW—salt water.
swab—a rod with rubber suction cups used inside the pipe.

swabbing—applying suction to draw fluid from the reservoir.
syncline—downwarped, usually trough-shaped rock formation.

T

T/—top of
TD—total depth.
term royalty—a royalty agreement limited by time or productivity.
test—the sampling of a reservoir.
tester—the person supervising drillstem-testing operations.
thribbles—drillpipe tubing when pulled from the well three joints at a time.
tight—nonporous.
tool pusher—drilling supervisor.
tour—work shift on a drilling operation (pronounced *tower*).
township—federal land survey consisting of sections of 36 square miles, numbered as to east-west and north-south coordinates.
TP—tubing pressure.
transfer order—an agreement to change production ownership.
trap—a geological barrier which prevents oil from flowing elsewhere.
truncation—a process of erosion.
tubing—removable pipe through which oil or gas flow or are pumped from a well.

U

unconformity—irregular erosion separating rock formations.
uplift—an area of geological elevation.

V

viscosity—the property of fluids by which they offer resistance to flow.

W

water cushion—water pumped into a drillpipe during production testing to prevent collapse due to sudden pressure changes.
wedge-out—edge of a lenticular rock formation.
wet gas—gas containing liquid hydrocarbons.
whipstock—a device used in drilling a hole at a slant.
wildcat—an exploratory well drilled in an area in which no oil or gas has previously been discovered.
windfall profits tax—an excise tax levied on oil production rather than profits.
WO/O—waiting on orders.
working interest—the mineral rights and obligations of the operator and his limited partners involving the cost of drilling and completion and the revenue from production.

Index

chart of wells - successes to date

Jay — investors references

lease info - copies of actual leases

copy operating agreement